A FIELD GUIDE TO

BANKSIAS

A FIELD GUIDE TO
BANKSIAS

IVAN HOLLIDAY
GEOFFREY WATTON

LANSDOWNE

Published by Lansdowne Publishing Pty Ltd
Level 5, 70 George Street Sydney NSW 2000, Australia

First published by Rigby Publishers 1975
Reprinted 1977

Second revised edition published 1990 by
Hamlyn Australia

Reprinted Lansdowne Publishing 1996 (limp)

Originated by Weldon Publishing
a division of Kevin Weldon & Associates Pty Limited

Edited by Roland Hughes
Designed by Christie & Eckermann, Art and Design Studio
Typeset in Australia
by Savage Type Pty Ltd, Brisbane
Printed in Singapore
by Kyodo-Shing Loong Printing Pte Ltd.

National Library of Australia
cataloguing-in-publication data:

Holliday, Ivan, 1926–
A field guide to banksias.

Rev. ed.
Includes index.
ISBN 1 86302 5022

1. Banksias — Australia. I. Watton, Geoffrey.

583. 9320994

Title page photograph:
B. ilicifolia.

CONTENTS

ACKNOWLEDGMENTS

In producing a book such as this, one must inevitably receive assistance from many people who have a special knowledge of the subject or can contribute in other ways.

The authors especially wish to express their appreciation to the following persons and organisations, without whose ready co-operation and assistance this publication would not have been possible:

Mr Ken Stuckey of Furner, Mrs Dulcie Rowley of Moorak, and Mr Eric Ashby of Inman Valley, all in South Australia, for making their fine collections of banksias available for inspection and photography when required by the authors.

Mrs Elaine Summers of Dongara, Mr and Mrs Don Bellairs of Kalbarri, and Mrs F. W. Humphreys of Perth, all in Western Australia; and the late Miss Alison Ashby of Adelaide, for their particular assistance with the locations of some of the rarer species in their wild habitat.

Others who assisted in providing material of some species or in other ways were Mr Fred Rogers of Melbourne, and Messrs Max Whiting, Lloyd Carman, and Don O'Brien of Adelaide. The latter's noteworthy contribution was a specimen of the northern *Banksia dentata* which he gathered during a visit to Cape York Peninsula.

The late Mr Rex Kuchel, formerly Assistant Director, the late Mr Ron Hill, technical assistant, and Mr Bruce Grivell of the Adelaide Botanic Garden, were invaluable in their willingness to assist at all times with technical queries. Also Dr Stephen Hopper of the Department of Conservation and Land Management and Mr I. R. Dixon of the Kings Park and Botanic Garden, both in Perth, Western Australia.

The ready assistance of the staff of the State Herbariums of South Australia, New South Wales, Queensland, and Western Australia is also acknowledged.

Photographic acknowledgment goes to the late Ron Hill (*Banksia attenuata, blechnifolia, canei, dentata, spinulosa* var. *collina*), Bruce Grivell (*B. lullfitzii*), Don Bellairs (*B. lindleyana*), Peter Taylor (*B. oligantha*), John Falconer (*B. epica*), Greg Keighery (*B. chamaephyton* and *B. oligantha* — fruit) and David Hockings (*B. plagiocarpa*).

Introduction

This book should be a useful guide for the trained botanist, but more particularly it is written for the ever-increasing number of people who are interested in Australian flora, and especially in banksias, one of the country's most attractive genus of plants.

At the time of this revision, discounting varieties and subspecies, there were 75 named species of *Banksia*. Of these, 61 (including *B. dentata*) were from Western Australia and the remainder from the eastern and southern States. One species, *B. dentata*, inhabits the north-west of Western Australia, the Northern Territory, and north Queensland, and extends to the islands of the Gulf of Carpentaria and New Guinea. It is certain that more revisions will be required from time to time as classification studies are undertaken and some name changes occur. Nature, however, is not concerned with the naming of plants, and field variations inevitably make it difficult to standardise a description of any one species. Sometimes these variations are treated as varieties of a particular species, or, rarely, they may be named as new species. More often they are considered habitat variations or forms within the same species. Recent investigations have identified many natural hybrids, particularly in the eastern States e.g. between *B. robur* and *B. oblongifolia*.

The genus *Banksia* was named after Sir Joseph Banks, the famous British botanist. Banks, often called the 'father of Australian botany', accompanied Captain James Cook on his voyage of discovery to Australia in 1770. Banksias belong to the family Proteaceae, a large family of plants found mainly in the southern hemisphere, with its greatest development in Australia.

Once commonly known as Native Honeysuckles because of the attraction of the flowers to nectar-feeding birds, they are now more often referred to by the generic name and are called banksias.

Banksias are all woody plants varying considerably in size, shape, and habit. Sometimes reaching tree proportions of 15 m or more high, they are more commonly shrubs, ranging from large, medium, and small bushes down to completely prostrate plants where the branches grow just below or at ground level, supporting erect leaves and flower spikes.

The tree banksias are noted for their thick, rough-barked trunks and gnarled, low-branching habit, which is particularly characteristic of older, mature specimens. Many of the shrubby species are large, upright, and dense-growing bushes, often noted for the colour and beauty of their flower spikes. Predominantly plants of poor sandy soils, banksias are commonly found in sandy heathlands not far from the coast. Habitat varies, however, for banksias range from true coastal species — e.g. *B. integrifolia*, which grows almost to the edge of the sea — to those species growing in high altitude alpine conditions, high rainfall forest lands, and inland sand heaths where summers are hot and dry.

Banksias bear large, conspicuous, and sometimes spectacular flower spikes (inflorescences). It's the inflorescences which vary from spherical or globular to a long cylindrical shape. Each is made up of numerous tightly packed, spirally arranged flowers. (The exceptions are *B. cuneata*, *B. ilicifolia* and *B. oligantha*.)

The sessile flowers are attached to the woody axis of the spike (**rachis**), by a densely furry bract and two similar bracteoles. Structurally, each flower is made up of a **perianth** which is a long, narrow tube, connected at its base to the rachis, where it encloses a long, wiry **pistil**. The base of the pistil forms a single-celled **ovary** containing two seeds.

At the late bud stage the apex of the pistil (**style end**) remains captive within the swollen tip, or **limb**, of the perianth. As the flower opens, the perianth splits into four segments, or laminae, releasing the style end. When released, the **styles** remain permanently hooked on some species, on others they straighten out horizontally, or arch slightly upwards into an erect position.

Each boat-like **perianth limb** contains a sessile **anther** which sheds its pollen just before the flower opens, the pollen being received by the captive end, or **pollen presenter** of the style. The pollen presenter is a swelling, or sometimes a narrowing, of the style end and presents pollen to the various pollinators — birds, small marsupials and insects. Just above the pollen presenter the style end bears the **stigma**. It is a very small, barely visible, groove which admits the pollinated pollen into the style, and conveys it to the ovary.

A characteristic of banksias is that the released styles remain permanently hooked when the flowers open from the top of the spike first (the exception is the pendent-spiked *B. nutans*). Conversely, in the species where the styles straighten out, the flowers almost always open from the bottom of the spike first.

As the flowers die and wither the spikes develop into woody fruiting cones which, in most species, retain the dead floral parts for a considerable time. In many species these dead flowers partly conceal the woody seed follicles which form and remain embedded in the rachis. When opened the follicles exhibit two valves each containing a flat winged seed. These are notoriously difficult to extract from most species, heat being necessary for their release. Under natural conditions they may remain enclosed in the unopened follicles for many years until a bushfire causes their release and the subsequent regeneration of new plants. As well as regenerating from seed, a number of banksia species survive through a lignotuber — i.e. a conspicuous swelling of the main trunk at or below ground level bearing latent buds from which shoots emerge and enable the plant to recover after apparent destruction by fire (similar to a mallee eucalypt which may recover by the same method). Another survival method is the emergence, after fire, of shoots from buds located under the bark.

The fruiting cones in some species are quite unique as well as forming interesting and attractive additions to the plants (e.g. *B. laricina*, *B. candolleana*).

Although creamy-yellow or yellow are the most common colours of banksia flower spikes, many other beautiful colours and colour combinations occur. These range through bronze shades to vivid orange, bright scarlet, purplish-black, and the unusual purplish-green colouring of *B. praemorsa*. The perianth limbs are usually a different colour to that of the perianth tubes and the styles, this feature adding beauty and interest at the various stages of development of the flowering spikes, from early bud to the point when the styles are fully exposed.

Just as there is considerable variation in the form that individual banksias take, and in the colour and form of the inflorescences, leaf or foliage differences are also common. These may be small and heath-like (as in *B. ericifolia*), or large and leathery in texture, often with sharp teeth along the margins, or leaves deeply divided to the mid-rib, and of large dimensions (e.g. *B. grandis*). Mainly alternate, or crowded into whorls around the branchlets, the leaves of a number of species are noted for their whitish or silvery under-surface.

Although banksias are grown in many gardens and plantations far from their native habitat, as a group they have not proved reliable as cultivated plants. Generally they resent fertilisers, particularly superphosphate, and require light, well-drained, slightly acid or neutral soils. They are also susceptible to certain soil fungus diseases such as 'Jarrah dieback' (*Phytophthora cinnamomi*). There is still a great deal to be learned about their cultural requirements and study groups are currently collating material which should further the knowledge of growing *Banksia*, one of the most beautiful and sought after groups of Australian plants.

CULTIVATION OF BANKSIAS

Much has to be learned about the cultivation of banksias and the following factors are worth recording.

MOISTURE REQUIREMENTS: Most banksias are plants of fairly infertile sandy heathlands where their root system is able to easily penetrate to depths of permanent moisture. While a few species inhabit swampy conditions, and others low rainfall sands where the topsoil dries out completely during summer, all banksias like water, provided the soil drainage is good.

DRAINAGE: Good drainage is of prime importance with most species, and very often more important than soil type. On sloping, well-drained sites (600 mm rainfall), many banksias have proved successful on clay soils over limestone (rendzinas and terra rossas). On level sites where there is a poorly drained clay subsoil, few banksias have succeeded, even though raised sandy beds may have been specially prepared above the clay to provide surface drainage.

pH OF THE SOIL: Most banksias prefer soils which are slightly acid to slightly alkaline in reaction, approximately pH 6.5 to pH 7.5. Sandy soils in this range are to their liking, although these promote fungus diseases which can attack banksias, particularly the younger plants.

FERTILISERS: Fertilisers are best avoided when growing banksias, although most western species appreciate periodic dressings of iron (chelates or sulphate) applied to iron-deficient soils, such as most of the soils of the Adelaide plains.

TIME OF PLANTING: Banksias develop most of their new growth above the ground in late summer and autumn, but their root system beneath the ground surface grows mainly through the winter, or wet season. For this reason it is best to plant young seedlings in late autumn and allow them to establish a self-supporting root system until the next summer without artificial watering.

If a young seedling is planted out at the primary growth stage during spring or early summer it may collapse due to insufficient moisture. Conversely, too much water can promote fungus diseases such as collar rot which will also cause its death. Because it is not possible to be certain of a particular plant's water requirements, there is a great risk in spring and summer planting, even where the sites are well drained. On the other hand, at some locations where the rainfall is very high during winter and where the soil can become waterlogged, spring planting is probably safer.

Contrary to many other Australian plants, banksias are best grown in containers for two years or more until strong, woody plants are formed. They are then better equipped at the planting-out stage to combat fungus and other diseases, to which young plants are particularly prone.

PLANTING SITE: Banksias prefer a sheltered site among other shrubby species which provide protection, shade, and a natural leaf mulch for their surface roots. However, planting in ground which is over-topped by established trees is generally best avoided.

p left: *Banksia ashbyi*. Top right: *B. prionotes*. Centre left: *B. laevigata*
osp. *fuscolutea*. Centre right: *B. ornata*. Bottom left: *B. candolleana*. ,
ttom right: *B. audax*.

B. aculeata A. S. George

DESCRIPTION: A dense, bushy shrub to 2 m high with very prickly foliage. The shrub has no lignotuber.

The specific name refers to the sharp-pointed leaf lobes.

Leaves: Broadly linear to narrowly cuneate with very sharp lobes. They are 4–9 cm long and up to 30 mm broad, channelled with rigid teeth up to 10 mm long. New growth is soft, bronze-green and hairy. The smaller branchlets are rusty-hairy grading to smooth and grey as they mature.

Flowers: The inflorescences hang downwards within the foliage and resemble those of *B. caleyi* and *B. lemanniana* in the habit of growth. Perianths are pink or purplish at the base grading to a pale greenish-cream, glabrous, with a keeled limb. Styles are cream and remain straight after being released. The flower spikes are cylindrical 6–9 cm long by 8–9 cm wide when fully mature. Flowering usually occurs in late summer to early autumn.

Fruits: The large fruiting cones, similar in size and shape to the flower spikes, contain many large dimpled follicles, up to 20 per cone. As the shrub has no lignotuber, it depends on regeneration from the seed contained in these follicles, after bushfires.

DISTRIBUTION: This species is endemic to the Stirling Ranges in southern Western Australia, where it favours gravelly or shaly sands. Rainfall is about 600 mm annually.

CULTIVATION: This species succeeds in well-drained soils in an open sunny position. Large bushes are growing in the deep grey sand adjacent to the Happy Valley Reservoir near Adelaide.

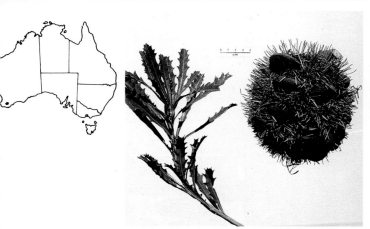

B. aemula R. Br.

WALLUM BANKSIA

DESCRIPTION: Previously known as *B. serratifolia*, Wallum Banksia is so closely related to the Saw Banksia (*B. serrata*) that the only significant difference is in the shape and size of the tiny pollen presenter at the end of the styles. Although more often a spreading shrubby species, due mainly to its sand-dune habitat, it also grows to a small, gnarled, and twisted tree where conditions are more favourable. Its red-grained timber and dark grey, rough bark, which wears to an orange-red, are also identical to those of the Saw Banksia. It has a lignotuber and after fire, may sprout from epicormic buds.

The specific name refers to the shrub's similarity to *B. serrata*, *aemulus* meaning like or equalling.

Leaves: These are narrowly obovate, leathery, with coarse, evenly serrated margins, parallel transverse veins, and green on both surfaces. Glossy above, the under-surface is paler green, usually coated with a grey or brownish down but is sometimes almost glabrous. They are commonly narrower (1–2 cm wide) than those of *B. serrata*, and the young leaves are a rusty brown.

Flowers: The flower spikes are very close to those of *B. serrata*, but are shorter and more squat. The styles are a similar yellow and the perianth limb a greyish or whitish-green. Their main difference is in the blunt pollen presenter which is smaller — about 1 mm long and cone-shaped. When released, from the bottom of the spike first, the thick styles curve slightly upwards.

The main flowering time is in late summer and autumn, but is irregular.

Fruits: Again these resemble those of *B. serrata*, being a thick spike with prominent, scattered, hairy, grey follicles which are hard, rounded and 2–3 cm broad. The tomentum rapidly wears off leaving the follicles smooth, while the old open follicles gape widely to expose a smooth interior.

DISTRIBUTION: This species is the dominant plant of much of southern Queensland's sandy coastal belt of lakes and dunes and is particularly common on Fraser Island. This part of Queensland is known as the Wallum, after the Aboriginal word for *B. serratifolia*. The plant extends well down the east coast to the Sydney region, always inhabiting sand-dunes or rocky headlands near the sea. Rainfall is 1000–1200 mm. In the Wallum area the period of maximum rainfall is summer.

CULTIVATION: Although not often cultivated, this species appears to require acid, well-drained, sandy or loamy soils, but according to its distribution should also withstand fairly boggy conditions.

n presenter enlarged

B. ashbyi E. G. Bak.

ASHBY'S BANKSIA

DESCRIPTION: The typical *Banksia* of the red sand country between Geraldton and Carnarvon in Western Australia, this species is usually a medium to large, upright and leafy shrub, 2–4 m high, but occasionally reaching small tree proportions. Most populations of this species are without lignotubers but recent investigation suggests that in its northern range, towards Exmouth, the plant develops lignotubers.

The specific name commemorates the late Edwin Ashby, a prominent South Australian native-plant enthusiast, whose daughter, the late Alison Ashby, is well known for her plant drawings for the South Australian Museum.

Leaves: The long, narrow, undulating leaves, 15–50 cm long by about 3 cm wide, are smooth on both surfaces, deeply lobed almost to the prominent yellow mid-rib, with distinct and intricate converging veins on the whitish-green under-surface. Each coarse, triangular lobe is sharply tipped, the younger leaves often with two prickly segments to each lobe.

Flowers: Ovoid to cylindrical, the large upright terminal flower spikes are 10–15 cm long by 7–10 cm in diameter, a rich glowing orange in colour. The flowers open from the bottom of the spike first, with no significant colour change, and the hairy perianth limbs are an apricot-orange. Styles are finally quite straight and horizontal, smooth, with a narrow, furrowed pollen presenter.

The main flowering period is in winter and each flower is long-lasting.

Fruits: Oblong to ovoid and usually narrower than the flower spikes, the fruiting cones retain the dead flowers which curl up between the follicles and then gradually wear off. Follicles are small, almost globular to ovoid, with a distinct suture. Furry at first, they soon wear smooth with age.

DISTRIBUTION: Commonly found in the Irwin, Austin, and Ashburton districts of Western Australia, this species grows in deep red sand in open, low-growing woodland or sand heath. Rainfall is 250–350 mm.

CULTIVATION: This is one of the most beautiful banksias for garden culture because of its ornamental, frond-like foliage and spectacular orange flower spikes which are much prized as cut flowers.

It requires a warm, open, well-drained site, preferably with a sandy topsoil. Slightly acid to slightly alkaline soils are best.

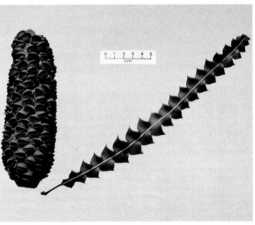

B. attenuata R. Br.

COAST BANKSIA, SLENDER BANKSIA

Description: Although there is a shrubby form with smaller flowers, this species is more often a small to medium-sized tree, 4–14 m high, with rough, dark grey bark and downy younger branches. It is inclined to grow erect with dense wide-spreading branches, but becomes more open as it ages. It has a lignotuber.

The specific name *attenuata* means 'narrowed', referring to the leaves, which taper narrowly to the base.

Leaves: These are broadly linear, wider towards the tip, 8–15 cm long by usually less than 1 cm wide, flat and stiff, evenly serrated and slightly prickly. The under-surface is usually white tomentose, with prominent, obliquely parallel, transverse veins.

Flowers: The cylindrical flower spikes are erect and terminate the branches. They are often very slender, up to 25 cm long, a very intense sulphur yellow in colour, and numerous. The bracts, which subtend the smooth individual flowers, are densely hairy. Styles are finally straight, and the pollen presenter is small and slender.

The main flowering period is October to March.

Fruits: Cones are long, narrow, and cylindrical; the ovoid to globular follicles prominent and covered with dense, grey, furry hairs. A distinctive feature is the way the dead flowers persist, but curl up like netting between the exposed follicles.

Distribution: Probably the most common *Banksia* throughout the south-west of Western Australia, usually found growing on deep, moist sands in heath or woodland, and sometimes the dominant tree within its habitat. It favours the wetter zones (rainfall more than 700 mm) but is also found in rainfall regions as low as 300 mm. It is a native of the Perth area.

Cultivation: This species requires acid to neutral, well-drained, light soil and assured moisture, but tolerates dry spells quite well.

B. audax C. A. Gardn.

DESCRIPTION: A rare species from the dry inland, this is a small, spreading, or sometimes upright shrub, usually under 1 m high by about the same width, often dome-shaped with many, fairly open branches. It has a lignotuber.

The specific name means 'bold' and may refer to the unusual and conspicuous two-toned inflorescences.

Leaves: The stiff, dull green, smooth but prickly leaves are narrowly wedge-shaped, 2–9 cm long by 6–12 mm wide, with small, fairly regularly serrated, sharp teeth, usually truncated at the apex. The mid-rib is prominent on both surfaces.

Flowers: Ovoid to cylindrical, the flower spikes are 9–13 cm long by 6–8 cm in diameter, erect on short branchlets and numerous. Their most distinctive feature is the curious colour combination of the dense woolly perianths. Beginning at the young bud stage as a rusty brown colour, they soon develop to small cylinders where the top and bottom colouring remains rusty brown, but the remainder of the spike becomes a creamy-buff colour. This colouring persists until the spikes are fully mature. The styles are smooth, bright yellow, finally straight and slightly upturned when released from the bottom of the spike first. The pollen presenter is narrowly cylindrical.

The flowering period is in summer.

Fruits: The fruiting cones are more or less egg-shaped with dark grey furry follicles completely hidden by the dead flowers which persist long after withering.

DISTRIBUTION: This is a low rainfall species (300–400 mm) from the eastern sand heaths of the Coolgardie–Southern Cross–Lake Grace district of Western Australia. Here it grows in open heathland where the sharp, white or yellow, sands are deep and very dry near the surface during summer months.

CULTIVATION: *B. audax* is not well known in cultivation, but its habitat suggests that it would be well-suited to a hot, dry climate (e.g. Adelaide) and well-drained, light soil conditions.

B. baueri R. Br.

POSSUM BANKSIA, WOOLLY-SPIKED BANKSIA

DESCRIPTION: A well-branched, rounded to dome-shaped, dense shrub to 2 m high by 3 m across, but sometimes growing up to 5 m high. It is distinctive because of its huge, soft, furry flower spikes which nestle in the foliage, often close to the ground, resembling small furry animals hiding within, which gives rise to the vernacular name. It has no lignotuber.

The specific name commemorates the nineteenth-century botanical artist Ferdinand Bauer.

Leaves: The rigid, prickly leaves are narrowly obovate, 7–13 cm long by 10–20 mm wide, glabrous, the margins evenly serrated with sharp-pointed teeth and the veins conspicuous on the under-surface.

Flowers: This species has the largest flower spikes of all the banksias. These are cylindrical, 15–40 cm long by 12–18 cm across, usually lemon-yellow at the base with long, woolly, grey-mauve tips. The perianth limb and tube is covered with long soft hairs and has an awn-like appendage at the end. Styles are finally straight. Colour variations occur from the usual subtle mauvish-grey and lemon, to a bright, tan colour form (from East Mount Barren). Flower spikes are generally upright on branchlets on the old wood, sometimes forming a mass within the centre of the plant. The flowering period is winter and spring.

Fruits: The withered grey perianths and styles remain almost indefinitely on the spike and virtually completely cover the furry, flattish seed follicles.

DISTRIBUTION: From the Stirling, Avon, and Eyre districts of Western Australia, it is a coastal or inland species, mainly from the open sand heaths on deep, white or yellow sand. It is also found on rocky sand at slight elevations — e.g. the Barren Ranges on the south coast. Rainfall is 350–650 mm.

CULTIVATION: A reasonably easy species to grow, favouring acid–neutral, light soils and needing little attention once established.

Its dense ground cover makes it a good plant for windbreak purposes. It is easily propagated.

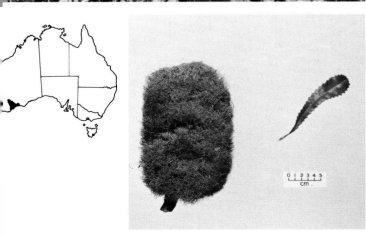

B. baxteri R. Br.

BIRD'S NEST BANKSIA, BAXTER'S BANKSIA

DESCRIPTION: A stout, single-stemmed, erect growing shrub with many, fairly open, nearly horizontal branches densely clad with deeply lobed, ornamental leaves. It matures to a wide dome-shaped shrub to 3 m or more high, without a lignotuber.

The specific name commemorates William Baxter, a nineteenth-century English gardener and botanical collector.

Leaves: Divided to the prominent yellow mid-rib into large triangular lobes with blunt ends that appear to be cut off. The rigid, slightly prickly leaves are a striking feature of the plant. 10–15 cm long by about 4 cm wide, they are dull green and smooth above, hairy beneath, but soon wearing smooth. The new growth is rust-coloured on reddish stems and the ends of the stiff branchlets bearing the flowers are clothed with long, feather-like hairs.

Flowers: Set in a rosette of new leaves, the erect, terminal yellow-green flower spikes are an ornamental feature when flowering. They are globular, or slightly dome-shaped, 6–10 cm long by about 8–12 cm in diameter. The erect styles are curved upwards at the base (incurved) and the perianths, styles, and bracts are covered with long, fine, feather-like hairs. The pollen presenter is narrow, furrowed, and without hairs. The flowering period is usually late spring and summer to early autumn.

Fruits: The cones are globular and flattish on top, the withered grey flowers remaining, giving the effect of a bird's nest set within the radiating leaves. Follicles are thick, furry, and prominent, the valves slightly lipped.

DISTRIBUTION: This species is common around King George's Sound and the flat sand heaths between the Stirling Ranges and the Pallinup River in Western Australia. Here it grows in open inland plains, near the coast, and frequently in marshy conditions in association with the Waratah Banksia (*B. coccinea*). It extends east of the Oldfield River in the Eyre district. Rainfall 500–700 mm.

CULTIVATION: An easy species to establish on light, acid–neutral soils, good as a windbreak and for cut flowers.

B. benthamiana C. A. Gardn.

DESCRIPTION: This rigid upright and prickly shrub reaches large proportions, 3–4 m high, with many erect branches and long stiff leaves. It has a lignotuber.

The specific name honours George Bentham, an English botanist of the nineteenth century noted for the monumental seven-volume work *Flora Australiensis.*

Leaves: Long and narrow, the leaves are usually 15–20 cm long by under 1 cm wide, glabrous, the bottom half of the leaf sometimes entire, with a few small, curved, sharp teeth at long intervals becoming more numerous near the acute apex. However, the leaves commonly bear teeth over their full length.

Flowers: The erect, intense golden flower spikes are produced throughout the shrub. They are cylindrical to ovoid, 7–12 cm long by about 6 cm in diameter, the bracts and perianths hairy and the styles smooth. When released, from the bottom of the spike first, the styles become erect, or incurved, with a long, narrow, furrowed, pollen presenter.

The flowering period is in summer. The shrub flowers at a very early age.

Fruits: These are the same size and shape as the inflorescences, the dead flowers persisting and mainly obscuring small flat densely furry follicles which barely protrude from the spike.

DISTRIBUTION: A dry area shrub of the Austin district of Western Australia it occurs in deep sandy heathland from Wilroy south to near Dalwallinu, where rainfall is about 300 mm annually.

CULTIVATION: This shrub is not well known in cultivation but succeeds in porous, well-drained soils in a dry or temperate climate.

B. *blechnifolia* F. Muell.

DESCRIPTION: A prostrate species with horizontal branches at ground level or just below, and vertically erect, handsome leaves and flower spikes. The branches may spread to about 2–3 m and sometimes fork towards the ends. It is without a lignotuber.

The specific name refers to the resemblance of the leaves to those of *Blechnum*, a genus of ferns.

Leaves: Quite variable, the large handsome leaves are 20–50 cm long by 4–12 cm wide, erect and usually smooth, divided virtually to the rigid and prominent mid-rib into individually variable segments. These are wing-shaped and entire, each lobe having three more or less parallel transverse veins and reticulate secondary veins. Young growth is bronze-red and velvety, the velvety hairs persisting on some leaves as they mature, but eventually wearing to a glabrous deep green. Branchlets are rusty-woolly.

Flowers: Flower spikes are borne erect at the ends of the creeping branches. Cylindrical, they vary in size from quite small spikes to more usually 10–15 cm long by 6–7 cm in diameter. Their colour is a dusky rose-red, the perianths silky hairy and the styles smooth, incurved, with a tiny yellow pollen presenter.

The flowering period is in spring and early summer.

Fruits: These are similar in size and shape to the flower spikes, the dead floral parts persistent. Follicles are prominent, flat, and densely furry.

DISTRIBUTION: A species that occurs mainly on open sand heath in the Stirling and Eyre districts of Western Australia. Rainfall is about 400 mm.

CULTIVATION: This species is a plant worth growing for its foliage alone. It has proved to be an adaptable plant provided it is given at least 40–50 cm of neutral to slightly acid sandy topsoil.

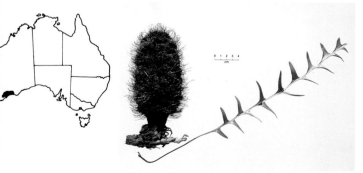

B. brownii Baxter ex R. Br.

FEATHER-LEAVED BANKSIA

DESCRIPTION: A rare, but ornamental, erect shrub, 2–6 m high, with smooth brownish bark and small, handsome, fern-like leaves. It usually branches near the base with foliage at ground level. It has no lignotuber.

The specific name honours a British botanist, Robert Brown, who was responsible for naming many other banksias.

Leaves: These are dainty and feather-like, with finely divided falcate segments reaching to the mid-rib, 7–12 cm long by 6–8 mm wide, bright green above with a white reverse, and soft to touch. The margins of the tiny segments are recurved and the mid-rib is raised prominently on the under-surface only. New foliage takes on a soft tan colour.

Flowers: Conspicuous and colourful, the cylindrical flower spikes are 10–20 cm long by 6–9 cm in diameter, a bright reddish, or sometimes a golden-brown colour, due to the various hues of the floral parts. The styles, which remain permanently hooked, are smooth and usually crimson grading to a cream colour at each end, the pollen presenter narrow. Perianths are hairy and a similar two-toned colour, or honey-coloured, while the unopened limbs are grey-brown. The flowers are arranged in vertical rows and open from the top of the spike first. It is usual for the new branches to radiate from just below the new flower buds which form at the tip of the previous season's growth. Flowers occur in autumn.

Fruits: Fruiting cones are narrow, the thin, flat, rounded, furry follicles almost hidden by the remaining dead floral parts.

DISTRIBUTION: This species is an inhabitant of rocky slopes in the Stirling Ranges and ranges south to near Albany in Western Australia. Away from the ranges it is found in finely textured sandy soils which remain wet in winter. Rainfall is 600–800 mm.

CULTIVATION: A fairly commonly cultivated shrub which adapts well in both full sun and shaded locations, provided the soil is acid–neutral, well-drained and moisture is assured. *B. brownii* responds well to cutting back and can be easily kept in shape.

B. burdettii E. G. Bak.

BURDETT'S BANKSIA

DESCRIPTION: One of the most ornamental of the shrubby banksias because of its flowers, this species is a fairly stiff, spreading shrub, 3–5 m high, often with a similar spread. It has no lignotuber.

The specific name commemorates William Burdett of Basket Range near Adelaide, who, with the Ashby family of Blackwood, have been noted for their pioneer work with native flora.

Leaves: 7–25 cm long by about 20 mm wide, the rigid, slightly twisted leaves are sharply and evenly toothed (teeth about 3 mm deep), narrowly cuneate to oblong in shape, but often notched at the tips. The young leaves are soft and woolly, greyish-green on both surfaces, but often mature to a glabrous upper surface. The under-surface has conspicuous oblique and parallel primary veins, and can be smooth but is more often covered with fine woolly hairs.

Flowers: A woolly grey-white in bud, the spikes become acorn-shaped as the flowers first open from the bottom, the soft white perianth limbs opening into a blaze of bright orange as the styles are released. Erect, and profuse, the spikes are ovoid-oblong when fully formed and usually 7–12 cm long by 8–10 cm in diameter. Perianths are villous, an apricot-orange in colour, and the styles are smooth and deep yellow with a paler yellow fusiform pollen presenter. When released the styles are erect and incurved. The flowering period is irregular, but usually occurs in late spring and summer, or early autumn.

Fruits: The cone is roughly ovoid and of similar size to the flower spikes. It retains the dead flowers which partly conceal the furry, rounded, but flattish seed follicles.

DISTRIBUTION: An inland species, it favours the well-drained sandy soils of the northern sandplains of Western Australia between Gingin and the Arrowsmith River. This country is essentially open woodland or sand heath with rainfall 550–600 mm.

CULTIVATION: This is a particularly ornamental species for both foliage and flowers. It prefers an open, well-drained site and needs little attention once established. It will withstand long dry periods very well.

B. caleyi R. Br.

CALEY'S BANKSIA

DESCRIPTION: A dense, rigid and prickly, well-branched shrub without lignotuber, its width is often greater than its height of 2–3 m. It is very similar to *B. lemanniana* and *B. aculeata*.

The specific name is in honour of George Caley, a nineteenth-century botanical collector.

Leaves: Hard, stiff, and prickly, the serrated leaves are roughly cuneate in shape, 5–10 cm long by 1–2 cm wide, with sinuate margins and a prominent mid-rib. The mature leaves are a dark glossy green, glabrous on both surfaces, but the young leaves are covered with soft brown hairs, giving to the new growth an attractive velvety bronze appearance.

Flowers: Unlike most other banksias, the flower spikes do not sit upright but are pendent (deflexed). Unfortunately they are mainly hidden within the dense foliage. When exposed they are most handsome, a dark scarlet or yellow in colour, the new spikes of the red form being particularly attractive because of the neat, spirally arranged, unopened, dark red perianth limbs. The spikes are 7–15 cm long by about 8 cm across, ovoid or globular, the perianths glabrous, and the styles finally straight and at right angles to the axis of the spike. The flowering period is long, usually spring to summer.

Fruits: Cones are pendent and globular with large prominent, egg-shaped follicles surrounded by the grey, withered flowers which remain for a considerable time, the styles projecting prominently. The grey follicles are densely furry, 2.5 cm wide by 1.5 cm thick.

DISTRIBUTION: Caley's Banksia is essentially an inland shrub of the gravelly sand heaths or open woodland of the Stirling and Eyre districts of southern Western Australia. Usually sandy, the soil is sometimes clay, but not limy, and rainfall is 550–600 mm.

CULTIVATION: Described as a hardy shrub by most writers, this species requires a well-drained light soil, pH 6.5–7.5. Once established it forms an excellent windbreak or screening shrub of ornamental appearance.

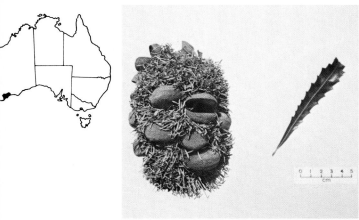

35

B. candolleana Meisn.

PROPELLER BANKSIA

DESCRIPTION: An unusual and extremely ornamental *Banksia* of semi-prostrate habit, spreading, and reaching about 1 m high, but sometimes growing slightly taller. Its branches tend to hug the ground but spread widely, the bush often covering an area greater than its height. It has a lignotuber.

The specific name honours a Swiss family of botanists, the De Candolle family.

Leaves: The long, narrow, erect leaves, which rise from low-set or underground branches, are 15–30 cm long by 6–8 mm wide, divided to the mid-rib into acutely dome-shaped lobes. The mid-rib is conspicuous and rigid, and the primary veins are prominent on the under-surface only.

Flowers: Almost globular, the flower spikes, which usually appear on the lower part of the branching stems, are small, only 5–6 cm in diameter, but often in clusters of two or three together. Before the smooth perianth limbs open, they are a light green colour, this feature enhancing the golden-orange of the other floral parts. In bud they are like small green pine cones. Perianths are villous (brownish hairs towards the tips) and the styles smooth with a light green, narrow, pollen presenter. The erect, incurved styles are released from the bottom of the spike first. Autumn and winter are the main flowering periods.

Fruits: Set in a small, globular cone, the huge, dull grey seed follicles are a distinctive feature because of their lateral beak which rather resembles a duck's bill. There are seldom more than two or three follicles on each cone. Often they resemble a ship's propeller.

DISTRIBUTION: This is a shrub of the sand heaths of the Irwin district of Western Australia, from Gingin northwards to the Arrowsmith River, where rainfall is 600–700 mm.

CULTIVATION: This attractive species requires an open situation on light sandy, well-drained, slightly acid to neutral soil. It is slow growing in cultivation.

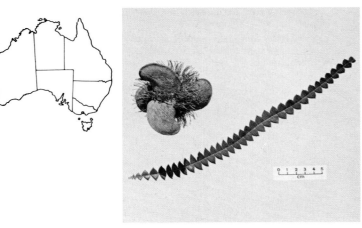

B. canei J. H. Willis

MOUNTAIN BANKSIA

DESCRIPTION: First described in 1967, Mountain Banksia is a relatively rare species from the rocky highlands of south-east Australia. It is a small, flat-crowned shrub 1–2 m or more in height, with attractive, usually prickly foliage. It probably has a lignotuber.

The specific name honours the late Bill Cane, a plant enthusiast and nurseryman from Maffra in the Gippsland area of Victoria.

Leaves: These are stiff and narrow, 2–7 cm long by usually less than 1 cm wide, relatively acute at the apex and sharply pointed, with long spiny teeth on the recurved margins, sometimes on one side of the leaf only or entire (in one form from Black Mountain, near Wulgulmerang). Generally the leaves are slightly curled, roughly oblong, with a prominent mid-rib bearing scattered rusty hairs and reticulate veins on the whitish under-surface. Young growth is golden bronze.

Flowers: The cylindrical inflorescences are small, usually under 10 cm long, their width about half their length. At the early bud stages and before releasing the styles, the hairy perianth limbs are a blue-grey colour, and with the yellowish-green unreleased styles and perianth tubes, they combine to produce a pleasing colour combination. When released, the smooth styles curve sharply upwards into an erect position.

The flowering period is in summer.

Fruits: The withered flowers soon fall and are always absent from the ovoid mature cones. The follicles are tightly compressed on the cone, densely hairy, the woolly hairs at first white, but maturing to dark grey with age.

DISTRIBUTION: This species has only been found in a few scattered locations in the high mountains of eastern Victoria and south-eastern New South Wales — e.g. near the upper Mitta Mitta and Wellington Rivers in the Victorian Alps and Wadbilliga Trig, Tuross Falls and Kydra Reefs in New South Wales. Wherever it occurs, however, it is locally abundant. It inhabits rocky or gravelly soils at altitudes of 1000–1500 m.

Climate is cold for most of the year with mild summers, and rainfall is 1000–1200 mm.

CULTIVATION: Mountain Banksia is suited to a well-drained, but moist situation in acid soils. Stratification of seed is necessary for germination.

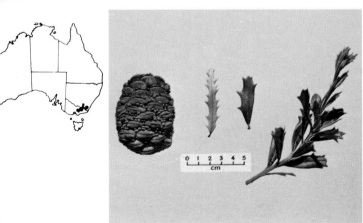

39

B. chamaephyton A. S. George

DESCRIPTION: One of the prostrate banksias with spreading branches at or below ground level, each branch supporting erect leaves and flower heads. The species has a lignotuber below the ground from which regrowth appears following bushfires.

The specific name is derived from the Greek, meaning a low-growing or prostrate plant.

Leaves: These are erect, 20–50 cm long and 4–15 cm wide, virtually divided to the mid-rib into linear lobes. Juvenile leaves are not so deeply divided. The underside of the leaves and the younger branches are covered with furry rusty hairs (tomentose).

Flowers: Terminal, cylindrical flower spikes rise vertically from the ground-hugging branches. These are 6–12 cm long, 5–7 cm in diameter, the perianths covered with long hairs on the outside. Perianths are cream with a brown limb and the styles are cream. Flowers usually appear in late spring.

Fruits: The dead flowers remain on the fruiting cone which contains up to 15 prominent egg-shaped follicles housing the seed.

DISTRIBUTION: Native to the sand heaths north of Perth, Western Australia, on deep sand over laterite. Its distribution is roughly the same as that of *B. burdettii*, from Eneabba to the Moore River, and the shrub is the only prostrate species from the northern sand heaths. Rainfall is 550–600 mm.

CULTIVATION: Relatively easy to grow in sandy or very well-drained soils, but it is slow growing. Somewhat similar to *B. blechnifolia* but not as ornamental in flower as that species.

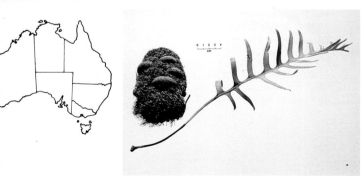

B. coccinea R. Br.

SCARLET BANKSIA, WARATAH BANKSIA, ALBANY BANKSIA

DESCRIPTION: One of the best-known banksias because of its spectacular inflorescences, the Scarlet Banksia is usually a tall, erect, but slender shrub with several upright main stems to 4 m or more high. Sometimes it grows to small tree proportions where conditions favour larger growth. The branches are densely coated with short, soft, matted fur. It has no lignotuber.

The specific name refers to the scarlet flower spikes (inflorescences), which are used extensively in the cut-flower trade.

Leaves: These are short and broad on short, thick stalks, 5–9 cm long by 4–7 cm wide, oblong or oval in shape, rigid, leathery, and bordered by small, irregular, prickly teeth. The under-surface is white or greyish, the veins and mid-rib prominent with the primary veins obliquely parallel.

Flowers: Unusual and beautiful, the flowering spikes are terminally erect and set in a rosette of leaves. They are squat, 6–12 cm long by 6–15 cm or more in diameter, usually wider than their length and cylindrical in shape. The flowers are carried in pairs in regular vertical rows so arranged that they resemble fine crochet work. The soft, furry, grey-white perianth limbs, hairy bronze perianth tubes, and bright scarlet, smooth styles, tipped with a conical golden pollen presenter, provide a lovely colour combination. When all the styles are finally released they are straight and long and obscure the grey perianth limbs.

The flowering period is from winter to summer, but continuing to the autumn in mountain habitats.

Fruits: The small, narrow ovoid cones contain very small, thin seed follicles which scarcely protrude from the cone. The seeds are notoriously difficult to extract.

DISTRIBUTION: This is a plant of the south coast of Western Australia, extending from just west of the Stirling Ranges to the Young River. Here it is common around the coast near Albany and in parts of the Stirling Ranges on a variety of gravelly, sandy or marshy soils and is at its best in moist, sheltered locations. Rainfall is 600 mm to over 800 mm.

CULTIVATION: This species has proved to be tricky in cultivation but has succeeded in well-drained acid soils which receive a high winter rainfall (e.g. parts of the Mount Lofty Ranges and the south-east of South Australia) although it can become quite dry in summer. Its shape can be improved by judicious pruning, with a resultant increase in flower spikes.

B. conferta A. S. George
var. conferta

DESCRIPTION: This mountain dwelling Queensland species is not well known. It is a tall, erect shrub or small tree to 4 m high with grey, tessellated bark and entire leaves resembling those of *B. integrifolia* to which it is related. Plants are probably killed by fire and regeneration is from seed.

The specific name refers to dense flowers in the spike, *confertus* meaning crowded.

Leaves: These are entire, elliptic to obovate, arranged in whorls around the branches, up to 12 cm long and normally, 1–4 cm wide. They are covered in white, furry hairs on the underside, with silky hairs above, grading to glabrous.

Flowers: Long, thin, cylindrical inflorescences are borne erect, usually within the foliage. These are bright golden when fully opened, up to 20 cm long by about 5 cm across. The perianths are pubescent on the outside, smooth within and the styles are pale yellow and remain straight after .being released. The flowering period is late autumn and winter.

Fruits: The fruiting cones resemble the inflorescence in shape, the dead flowers persisting for some time. Numerous, narrowly elliptic follicles are scattered throughout the cone.

DISTRIBUTION: Rocky, mountain areas of south-eastern Queensland, on the Lamington Plateau and the Glasshouse Mountains. Rainfall is 1000–1500 mm.

B. conferta var. ***penicillata*** A. S. George. Differs from var. *conferta* in its smooth bark, villous new growth, often serrated leaves, tufts of hairs on the apices of the common bracts subtending flower-pairs (from which the variety name is derived), and in its slightly larger follicles. It is found only in the Blue Mountains of New South Wales, an outlier also occurring north of Bowral, usually in open forest near cliffs. Flowering occurs from autumn through winter.

CULTIVATION: The authors have had limited experience with these two banksias, although young plants are reported to be growing well in Perth (var. *conferta*), the National Botanic Gardens, Canberra (var. *penicillata*) and adjacent to Mount Gambier, South Australia (both varieties).

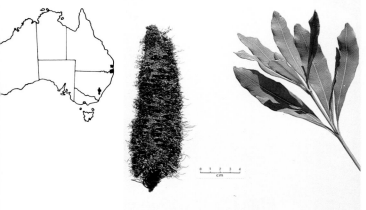

45

B. cuneata A. S. George

MATCHSTICK BANKSIA

DESCRIPTION: A fairly spindly erect shrub or small tree reaching about 5 m high at its best. Bark is smooth and grey, hairy on the smaller branchlets, and the foliage is prickly. The species has no lignotuber, depending on regeneration from the seed after fire.

The specific name refers to the wedge-shaped leaves.

Leaves: These are scattered, 1–4 cm long by 5–15 mm wide, wedge-shaped, serrated, with very sharp teeth. They are hairy (hirsute) becoming glabrous on the top side, the pits on the lower surface being woolly.

Flowers: Attractive pink and cream inflorescences are prominently displayed in heads at the ends of the branches. The unopened perianths are pink with greenish-cream limbs, each perianth resembling a matchstick, hence the common name of this species. Perianths are silky hairy on the outside. Young styles are cream but age to a reddish colour.

Flowering occurs in spring from September to December.

This species is related to *B. ilicifolia* and *B. oligantha* in having flower heads more like those of Dryandra than the characteristic spike of the banksias.

Fruits: Only one to three follicles form after flowering and are obliquely ovoid in shape and mottled grey in colour.

DISTRIBUTION: *B. cuneata* is found in deep sand in heath or low woodland in the area between Brookton and Bruce Rock in Western Australia. Annual rainfall is 400 mm.

CULTIVATION: This is an ornamental species which has horticultural potential, but is seldom cultivated. Since it grows in close association with *B. prionotes* it should prosper in an open sunny situation with well-drained soils.

B. dentata L.f.

TROPICAL BANKSIA

DESCRIPTION: A northern monsoonal tree, this species is the only *Banksia* to be found outside Australia, extending to New Guinea. It is usually seen as a small, scraggy, sparsely branched tree, 5–8 m high, with divaricate branches and dark grey, rough bark. The inner bark is blood red. Timber is dark red, hard, close-grained, and attractive. It has a close affinity with the Coast Banksia (*B. integrifolia*) although its leaves are noticeably different.

Its specific name refers to the leaf margins which are dentate.

Leaves: The large irregularly or sometimes regularly toothed leaves are 10–25 cm long by 2–8 cm wide, cuneate-oblong to elliptic with short stalks, the margins slightly recurved. The under-surface is white and tomentose, the oblique and parallel primary transverse veins more prominent than those of *B. integrifolia.*

Flowers: The inflorescences are usually a little larger than those of *B. integrifolia*, but otherwise identical. They are pale yellow in colour, cylindrical, the style finally straight or slightly curved and spreading with a narrow pollen presenter. Perianths are silky hairy.

Flowers occur throughout autumn and winter — the dry months of the northern areas.

Fruits: The withered flowers soon fall to leave a narrow, white, tomentose spike exposing thin-valved, scattered follicles. Seeds are ejected as soon as they are ripe.

DISTRIBUTION: A monsoonal species found in open sclerophyll forest of the northern coastal fringe extending from Western Australia through central Australia to Queensland, usually on sand near swamps. It also grows on the islands of the Gulf of Carpentaria and in New Guinea. Climate is one of very high summer rainfall, but relatively dry winters.

CULTIVATION: It is unknown in the southern temperate regions.

B. dryandroides Baxter ex Sweet

DRYANDRA-LEAVED BANKSIA

DESCRIPTION: A dense, low, spreading, dome-shaped shrub which is noted for the beauty of its ferny, dryandra-like foliage. It seldom grows any taller than about 1 m high with a spread sometimes twice its height. It has no lignotuber.

The specific name refers to the leaves which resemble those of some species of the related genus, *Dryandra.*

Leaves: These are 5–15 cm long by about 1 cm wide, divided to the mid-rib by neat, regularly spaced, triangular segments, which are at right angles to the stem, acuminate, with recurved margins. They are concave and bright green above, the reverse side white, but the mid-rib covered with soft, brown hairs. The small branches and new leaves are also covered with dense, brown hairs which enhance the foliage effect of the plant.

Flowers: The ovoid-globular flower spikes on short, lateral branches are upright, about 4 cm in diameter, but well hidden within the foliage. Their colour is an amber or brownish shade and not conspicuous. The styles remain hooked after the perianths have opened. Flowering is profuse, occurring mainly in spring and summer. Some flowers are present most months.

Fruits: The cones are quite distinctive, about 4–5 cm long and often slightly wider than their length, the follicles numerous, narrow, and prominent, at first covered with brown hairs but soon wearing partly smooth to display a wavy brown suture. In general appearance they bear some resemblance to the unique fruits of *B. laricina* but are much darker in colour with less conspicuous follicles.

DISTRIBUTION: A species of fairly restricted distribution in the Stirling Ranges, Western Australia, from Mount Manypeaks near Albany and extending about 160 km to Bremer Bay in the east. The soil is sandy or gravelly and rainfall is 700–800 mm.

CULTIVATION: Often cultivated for its foliage, this species forms a lovely rock garden or foreground shrub which requires acid, well-drained soils high in iron if it is to succeed.

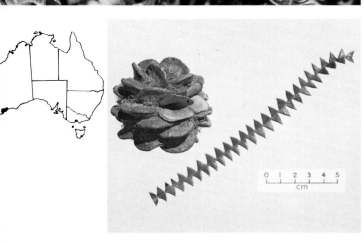

B. elderiana F. Muell. and Tate

PALM BANKSIA, SWORDFISH BANKSIA

DESCRIPTION: A dense, many-stemmed shrub, 1–3 m high with similar spread, distinctive because of its very long, narrow, and sharp-pointed leaves. It has a lignotuber.

The specific name is in honour of Sir Thomas Elder who sponsored several botanical expeditions in Australia during the nineteenth century.

Leaves: These are particularly long, sometimes in excess of 50 cm, and narrow, 1–1.5 cm wide, rigid, with widely-separated teeth (2–3 cm apart). The teeth are curved and very sharp, their depth over halfway to the mid-rib, which is yellow and prominent. Both surfaces are smooth, the veins on the under-surface reticulate, and the attractive young growth a hairy rusty green.

Flowers: Ovoid or oblong, the handsome bright yellow flower spikes are pendent on short branchlets on the old wood. They are about 10–12 cm long by 7–10 cm in diameter, the released styles finally very straight and at right angles to the axis of the spike. Styles are smooth with a long furrowed pollen presenter and the perianths hairy. The flowering period is summer to early autumn.

Fruits: These are similar in size and shape to the flower spikes, the follicles ovoid, about 2 cm wide by 1 cm thick, densely hairy and well hidden by the persistent dead floral parts.

DISTRIBUTION: A dry area species from the Austin, Coolgardie, and Eyre districts of inland Western Australia, it can be found growing in sand or sandy loam on open plain country. Rainfall is 200–400 mm. A fairly common shrub along the roadsides, east and north of Lake King.

CULTIVATION: This species has been successfully grown in areas of much higher winter rainfall — e.g. Kings Park, Perth, and the Adelaide Hills (rainfall 700 mm or more) — provided the drainage is good. It is an ornamental, but very prickly shrub.

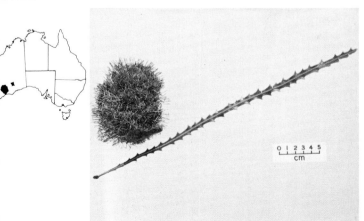

53

B. elegans Meisn.

ELEGANT BANKSIA

DESCRIPTION: A very rare plant of the sand heaths south of Geraldton, this species is usually a gnarled and thick-trunked, spindly shrub, 2–3 m high, but specimens of small tree proportions are known. Bark is thick, grey, and mottled. It has a lignotuber and after fire or root damage there is evidence of root suckering.

This species is noted for its graceful, wavy, bluish-grey foliage, from which it derives its specific name.

Leaves: Occurring mainly at the ends of the branches, the prickly leaves are long, 15–30 cm by about 1.5–2 cm wide, glaucous, and divided about one third of the way to the mid-rib by regular, triangular, sharp-pointed lobes. They are often curled or wavy, the mid-rib prominent on both surfaces and the under-surface clothed with a minute whitish tomentum.

Flowers: Erect inflorescences set within the leaves are more or less dome-shaped (globular), 5–7 cm in diameter and resemble the heads of drumsticks. The very long rigid perianths, consisting of square-sectioned, minutely hairy, yellow tubes, tipped with darker greenish-blue or pale green limbs, are like matches projecting from the rachis. The tiny yellow smooth styles do not project beyond the perianth limbs as the flowers open. The flowering period is in spring and early summer.

Fruits: The small fruiting cones consist of a smooth grey rachis from which arise usually only one, but sometimes several conspicuous almond-shaped follicles. Although smaller, the fruits resemble those of *B. candolleana*, but the follicles are without the prominent lateral beak, and are stippled with numerous tiny white projections.

DISTRIBUTION: This species can still be found growing in very deep, poor, white sand, confined to the Eneabba–Dongara area of the Irwin district of Western Australia. The climate is dry and the soil well-drained, and rainfall is 500–600 mm.

CULTIVATION: This shrub has only recently been introduced to cultivation and the authors are not aware of any mature specimens. Seed is difficult to procure at present, and this restricts its cultivation.

B. epica A. S. George

DESCRIPTION: A dense, bushy and spreading shrub to 2 m high by 2–3 m wide, without a lignotuber, and with closely hoary branchlets. It has similarities to the better known *B. media*, with which it associates under natural conditions.

Its specific name refers to the epic journey from South Australia to Western Australia of Edward John Eyre, who allegedly first saw this banksia in 1841, although it was only first collected in 1973 by Charles Nelson. In 1985, John and Lalarge Falconer collected and recognised it as a distinct species, and it was named by Alex George in 1987.

Leaves: These are 15–50 mm long by 6–15 mm wide, obovate to narrowly cuneate, truncate, the margins flat or slightly recurved with short serrations or occasionally entire. They are noticeably smaller than those of *B. media*. The upper surfaces are rusty-tomentose and the under-surfaces reticulate and woolly.

Flowers: These occur in pale to mid-yellow cylindrical spikes up to 17 cm long, but usually less, by about 6 cm wide. The cream styles project outwards and upwards and the straight perianths are pubescent on their upper half but smooth over the lower half of the tube. Flowering occurs mainly from April to June.

Fruits: The long cones are about the same size as the flower spikes and can be easily distinguished from those of *B. media* by their covering of numerous, persistent, curled and ascending styles which frequently obscure the smooth and dimpled seed follicles for several years. The dead styles of *B. media* hang downwards.

DISTRIBUTION: So far, only known from two locations in Western Australia, Toolinna Cove and 30 km west of Point Culver, along the coastline of the Great Australian Bight where it grows in sandy heathland over limestone cliffs in association with *B. media* and *B. speciosa*.

CULTIVATION: Unknown in cultivation (1988) but it should succeed where *B. media* and *B. speciosa* are successful.

B. ericifolia L.f.
var. *ericifolia*
HEATH-LEAVED BANKSIA

DESCRIPTION: Usually a compact, tall, and shapely shrub to 7 m high without a lignotuber and with branches to near ground level. It is frequently cultivated and is the most colourful of the eastern species when in flower. Bark is grey-brown and generally smooth, but with small, horizontal, rough patches on the main trunk and larger branches.

This species is allegedly the first specimen collected by Sir Joseph Banks at Botany Bay in 1770. Its specific name refers to the distinctive heath-like foliage (i.e. like that of an *Erica*).

Leaves: These are crowded, small, 10–20 mm long, and narrow (linear) with notched ends (retuse). The edges are entire with closely revolute margins, the colour dark green but much paler when young.

Flowers: Orange-red in colour, the cylindrical flower spikes are spectacular at their best, usually in winter. Long and narrow, up to 30 cm long by about 5 cm in diameter, they first open from the top of the spike, which is characteristic of banksias in which the style remains hooked. The smooth style is permanently hooked at the tip and the perianth covered with yellow silky hairs. The flowering period is late autumn to spring.

Fruits: Long and narrow, the fruiting cones are oblong-cylindrical containing nut-like follicles which are wide and rather flat with a prominent suture. The styles soon fall but the dead perianths remain on the spike where the follicles have not formed.

DISTRIBUTION: A widely-distributed shrub of the sandy central coastal regions and nearby mountains of New South Wales, common around Sydney and in the Blue Mountains. Rainfall is 800–1300 mm.

CULTIVATION: Well known in gardens, this species has proved fairly adaptable in cultivation, but requires a well-drained acid soil for reliable results. The flowers are full of nectar and very attractive to native birds.

B. ericifolia L.f. var. ***macrantha*** A. S. George. This variation of Heath-leaved Banksia comes from the north coast of New South Wales in two disjunct populations between Murwillumbah and Taree. It differs in the more crowded, narrower leaves, longer perianths with hirsute limb and longer pistils. The shrub favours deep sand, sometimes swampy flats mainly within 2 km of the coast.

B. gardneri A. S. George
var. *gardneri*

DESCRIPTION: A shrub of quite prostrate habit with spreading branches on the ground surface and erect leaves and flower spikes. It has a lignotuber.

The specific name honours Charles Gardner, a former Government Botanist (from 1929 to 1960) of Western Australia.

Leaves: These are erect, scattered, 10–40 cm long by 2–8 cm wide, deeply lobed, the lobes triangular to broadly linear, obtuse or acute, and deep green. New growth is a rusty red and covered with long soft hairs (villous), the leaves tending to lose these hairs as they age.

Flowers: The flower spikes are erect at the ends of the creeping branches, sometimes several together, cylindrical, usually 7–12 cm long by 6–8 cm in diameter. Perianths are a rusty brown colour, sometimes a pale brown, densely hairy (hirsute) with the limb becoming glabrous except at the apex. The styles are smooth and yellow with a small narrow pollen presenter. They open from the bottom of the spike first. It flowers in spring.

Fruits: The fruiting cones are the same size and shape as the inflorescences, with flat, elliptic, and furry follicles. The dead flowers are persistent.

DISTRIBUTION: A plant of the sandy or gravelly shrub and woodlands of south-west Western Australia extending from north of Denmark to Bremer Bay and south towards Albany. Annual rainfall is 600–800 mm.

***B. gardneri* var. *hiemalis* A. S. George.** Another variety differing in its pale green leaves and pink perianths with a pale brown limb. It flowers in winter, a feature from which the variety name is derived. This variety is mainly found further to the east between Harrismith, West Mount Barren and Ravensthorpe.

***B. gardneri* var. *brevidentata* A. S. George.** A similar prostrate shrub with short toothed (dentate) leaves and winter flowering period. It is restricted to the Stirling Ranges and a single occurrence near Albany. Recent investigations (1988) have located a population some 30 km west of Cranbrook (Warrinup Reserve).

CULTIVATION: Each of these varieties is relatively easy to grow if given a light well-drained acid to neutral soil and moderate rainfall. They make good rock garden subjects.

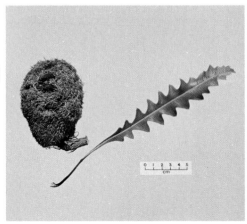

B. goodii R. Br.

DESCRIPTION: One of the western prostrate banksias which has spreading branches either below or just above the ground, and erect leaves and flower spikes. Although completely prostrate with creeping stems, they are true shrubs with a long life. It has a lignotuber.

B. goodii is a very rare species which faces extinction in its wild habitat. It bears a close resemblance to another prostrate species, *B. gardneri*, the main differences being in the leaves and the long, villous bracts at the base of the flower spikes.

Its specific name honours an early Australian plant collector, Peter Good, who accompanied Robert Brown on the *Investigator*.

Leaves: These are erect, almost at right angles to the prostrate stems, forming a circle surrounding the flower spikes. They are large, 25–45 cm long by about 3–7 cm wide, roughly oblong-ovate, tapering to a thin stalk which is arranged spirally on the branch. The margins are undulate or sinuate, irregularly to regularly toothed with sharp curved teeth, the transverse veins obliquely parallel and conspicuous on both surfaces. The mid-rib is yellow and prominent and both surfaces are coated with short woolly hairs. Young growth is greyish and softly hairy.

Flowers: The flowering spikes emerge vertically erect from the ends of the creeping stems, up to 20 cm long by about 7 cm in diameter, ovoid to cylindrical. The individual flowers are packed so tightly that the spikes resemble bronze velvet before the styles are released. The very small yellow styles curve upwards when released. The flowering period is in late spring and early summer.

Fruits: These are similar in size and shape to the flower spikes, the dead flowers remaining. Seed follicles are prominent, densely furry, and brown in colour.

DISTRIBUTION: This species is so rare that it is only known from a few isolated sandy roadsides east and west of the Albany Highway just north of Albany in agricultural areas. Rainfall is about 800 mm.

CULTIVATION: Because of its rarity, the seed of *B. goodii* is difficult to obtain. A few enthusiasts have grown this species with some success on soils which have a sandy topsoil to at least 30 cm depth. It makes an excellent rock-garden subject.

B. grandis Willd.

GIANT BANKSIA, BULL BANKSIA

DESCRIPTION: A small upright tree seldom exceeding about 8 m in height, with rough, grey bark and foliage much denser at the ends of the spreading branches. In its young stages it grows very straight and upright, and with its large, radiating leaves and red, woolly new growth at the top, reminds one of a tropical hot-house plant. It appears to have a lignotuber and after fire usually shoots from epicormic buds.

The specific name means 'tall' or 'large', possibly referring to the inflorescences which are particularly long and upright, or to both the flower spikes and the leaves.

Leaves: Huge, shining, dark green leaves, 20–50 cm or more long, are deeply divided almost to the mid-rib into large, roughly triangular lobes which are larger near the middle of the leaf, each lobe overlapping the preceding one. The leaves form a circle around the flower spikes and their under-surface is coated with a soft, white tomentum, with transverse veins and yellow mid-rib prominent. The young leaves and branches are a particularly attractive soft woolly bronze or red colour.

Flowers: The inflorescences resemble huge golden-yellow candles, standing erect above the foliage. They are cylindrical, sometimes exceeding 40 cm in length, but more commonly 25–30 cm long by about 10–12 cm wide. The long styles are tipped with a small, oblong pollen presenter and remain curved but not hooked. *B. grandis* flowers in the spring and early summer.

Fruits: The large fruiting cones are cylindrical and usually characterised by a blunt cone at the apex where the seed follicles have not formed. The dead flowers soon fall off leaving many sharp, thin follicles.

DISTRIBUTION: One of the most common western banksias, this tree is encountered mainly as an understorey tree in eucalypt forest in both the lateritic gravelly soils of the Darling Range and in wet sandy soils of the Jarrah and Karri forests. It also extends some distance north of Perth and is found in a stunted form on granite rocks and limestone cliffs of the south and west coast extending east to Cape Riche. Rainfall is 700 to more than 1400 mm.

CULTIVATION: A particularly ornamental tree because of its foliage as well as its flowers, this species can be grown in shade and open situations. It requires acid to neutral, well-drained soils, with adequate moisture.

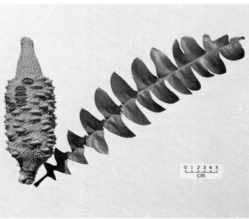

B. grossa A. S. George

DESCRIPTION: One of several shrubs previously assigned to the *B. sphaerocarpa* group, it grows to an open bush about 1 m high with a lignotuber. The bark is a flaky brown.

The specific name refers to the thick leaves, flowers and follicles, *grossus* meaning 'coarse' in Latin.

Leaves: These are linear and scattered, 4–12 cm long by 2–3 mm wide with revolute margins. They are silky hairy to smooth on the upper surface but woolly below.

Flowers: The inflorescences are barrel-shaped, a golden-brown in colour, and set on short lateral branches within the bush, although sometimes they terminate the main branches. The perianth is hairy (hirsute) both outside and inside and the styles are often a deep red in colour and permanently hooked after being released. Flower spikes are up to 7 cm long. Flowers are produced in the autumn (March) and carry on into early spring.

Fruits: Similar in shape to the flower heads, these bear large elliptical hairy follicles with the dead flowers persisting around them.

DISTRIBUTION: This is one of the more northern of the banksias from Western Australia, inhabiting shallow or deep sand over laterite in shrubland from the Eneabba to Regans Ford areas. Annual rainfall is about 600 mm.

CULTIVATION: A slow growing spreading shrub which prefers poor, well-drained soils in an open situation.

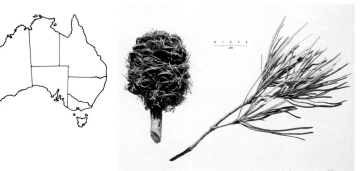

B. hookeriana Meisn.

HOOKERS' BANKSIA

DESCRIPTION: One of several particularly ornamental species, it grows into a dense and compact shrub, 2-3 m high with about the same spread. It has attractive foliage and flower spikes in great numbers. Bark is marbled, rough textured, a grey and orange colour, but furry grey on the young branchlets. It has no ligno-tuber.

The specific name honours the nineteenth-century British botanists William Jackson Hooker and his son Joseph Dalton Hooker.

Leaves: The smooth leaves are long and narrow, 10–25 cm long by about 1 cm wide, mainly truncate, and divided about halfway to the mid-rib by small, evenly-serrated teeth. The mid-rib is prominent and the under-surface woolly on the younger leaves.

Flowers: Short, thick, cylindrical, terminal flower spikes, 8–10 cm by 6–8 cm across, are erect and very lovely at all stages of development. Before the spikes open they are a velvety white, due to the soft hairy perianth limbs. At this stage they resemble a lighted white lampshade, the subdued golden background caused by the colour of the villous perianth tubes. As the smooth styles are released the spikes become acorn-shaped, and a bright, golden-orange and white. Finally they turn completely orange. The released styles with a yellow pollen presenter are straight and point almost vertically upwards.

The flowering period is mainly winter to summer, but a few flowers carry on into the autumn.

Fruits: The cones are narrower than the flower spikes, cylindrical, usually about 4–5 cm in diameter. Follicles are flattish but roughly egg-shaped, not large, densely furry, the hairs quite long and projecting slightly from the spike. The dead flowers persist for a considerable time.

DISTRIBUTION: This shrub is a native of the Irwin district of Western Australia where it is inclined to grow in open thickets in light sandy soil. It is common around the Eneabba and Arrowsmith River area. Rainfall is 600 mm.

Much of its habitat is gradually disappearing as agricultural development extends into the area.

CULTIVATION: Hookers' Banksia requires a composted, slightly acid to neutral sand in an open situation for best results. It is a rapid grower under favourable conditions.

B. ilicifolia R. Br.

HOLLY-LEAVED BANKSIA

DESCRIPTION: This species with *B. cuneata* and *B. oligantha* are unique among the *Banksia* genus because of the inflorescences which form a rounded rosette encircled by the leaves rather than the typical cylindrical or globular spike. These resemble those of the genus *Dryandra*, but without the circle of bracts which surround the flower head. They possibly provide a link between these two genera.

Holly-leaved Banksia is usually a medium-sized tree, 7–10 m high, with a short, often crooked trunk and rough, furrowed, grey bark, although different forms occur. Near Perth it appears as an erect tree of cypress-like habit. It has a lignotuber and after fire may shoot from epicormic buds.

Both the specific and vernacular names refer to the holly-like leaves.

Leaves: These are a dark, glossy green, 6–10 cm long by 3–4 cm wide, obovate, the margins undulate, with irregular, small, prickly teeth, but sometimes these are absent. The leaves encircle the terminal flower spikes, giving a wreath-like effect.

Flowers: The inflorescences are in hemispherical globular heads, usually a lemon-yellow, but turning red with age, the two-toned effect contrasting well with the dark foliage. The perianth limbs separate as the tube opens, in contrast to other banksias where the limb remains coherent long after the tube splits. Flowers can occur at any time, although winter to early spring is the main flowering period.

Fruits: The hard follicles form on a very small cob, only two or three forming from any one flower head. These are roughly almond-shaped and covered with dense woolly hairs.

DISTRIBUTION: This is a species of the wetter sandy coastal plains of Western Australia which extend from Mt Lesueur in the north to Augusta in the south; and east to the Cordinup River, between Albany and Bremer Bay. It is a native of the Perth area. Rainfall is usually in excess of 700 mm.

CULTIVATION: Rarely cultivated, this species could be grown as an ornamental and unusual small tree on moist sandy soils.

B. incana A. S. George

DESCRIPTION: A low, spreading shrub usually under 1 m high, with a lignotuber and slightly glaucous, needle-like leaves. Previously included within the *B. sphaerocarpa* group, this newly named (1981) species is said to be the easiest to identify of three recently named similar small shrubs (*B. micrantha* and *B. sphaerocarpa* var. *sphaerocarpa*–northern form) that occur in the low heathlands in the vicinity of Mt Lesueur in Western Australia. Not always easy to separate, this species rapidly sheds its dead flowers. Its fruits are unique among these three in that the fruiting spikes are completely devoid of the remains of the dead flowers among the very large follicles.

The specific name is from *incanus* (hoary), referring to the closely pubescent grey follicles.

Leaves: Scattered, narrowly linear, acute leaves, 1–6 cm long and up to 2 mm wide appear on densely tomentose branchlets. These are pubescent, becoming glabrous on the upper surface, closely revolute, the concealed under-surface woolly. New growth is bright green.

Flowers: The erect inflorescences are spherical, up to 7 cm wide, on lateral branchlets, the flowers bright yellow, those towards the apex sometimes reddish, occasionally purple. Styles are yellow and after release from the perianths remain permanently hooked. Perianths are silky hairy outside, glabrous inside. Flowering period is from November to April.

Fruits: The dead flowers soon fall to reveal prominent, elliptic to rhomboid, hoary grey follicles.

DISTRIBUTION: This shrub is native to the northern sand heaths between Perth and the Arrowsmith River, commonest in the Mt Lesueur area in deep sand or sand over laterite in low woodland. Annual rainfall is 600–900 mm.

CULTIVATION: A shrub requiring deep sand or soil with very free drainage for best results.

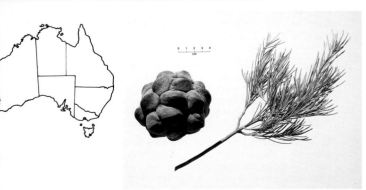

B. integrifolia L.f. var. *integrifolia*
COAST BANKSIA

DESCRIPTION: One of the largest and loveliest banksias, growing into a tree 10–20 m at its best. Particularly in exposed coastal locations, it often assumes twisted or gnarled shapes of rugged character. The bark is rough and light grey and old trees often support patches of moss and lichens which enhance its appearance. The young branches are covered with a white down. It has a ligno-tuber and, after fire, often shoots from epicormic buds.

The specific name refers to the entire or unbroken leaf margins which are characteristic of the species, although they sometimes occur in a toothed form on adult species.

Leaves: The adult leaves are mainly entire, but sometimes irregularly toothed, a dark glossy green in colour, but silver tomentose on the under-surface with conspicuous lateral veins and mid-rib. They are usually 5–15 cm long by 1–2 cm broad, in whorls, oblanceolate or narrowly elliptic in shape tapering to a short leaf stalk. Juvenile leaves are often irregularly toothed.

Flowers: Erect, terminal flower spikes are oblong or cylindrical, 7–15 cm long, their diameter about half their length. Pale yellow when young, they darken with age, becoming a bronze colour before dying. The style is finally straight and spreading with a small thin brown pollen presenter. The flowers open from the bottom of the spike first.

Flowering occurs throughout the year but mainly in autumn and winter.

Fruits: The withered flowers fall rapidly, leaving a clean, narrow, white or grey tomentose spike, the mature, thin-valved follicles protruding prominently. Seeds are freely ejected when ripe.

DISTRIBUTION: Perhaps the most common species of the east coast, this tree extends from Port Phillip Bay in Victoria to Fraser Island in Queensland. Within this range it grows to the water's edge where it is exposed to harsh sea winds which help to determine its size and often irregular shape. Rainfall is 700–1300 mm.

CULTIVATION: Coast Banksia adapts well to cultivation where soils are neutral-acid and well-drained, and rainfall is adequate (more than 500 mm). It is not suited to the exposed alkaline sand dunes of coastal Western and South Australia.

B. *integrifolia* L.f. var. *compar* (R. Br.) Bailey. Closely related to var. *integrifolia*, this tree differs in its larger, undulate leaves up to 20 cm long which are bright glossy green on the upper surface.

It is found in coastal Queensland as far north as Proserpine extending southwards to Mt Wilson in the Blue Mountains, and reaching altitudes of 1200 m in places such as Barrington Tops.

B. *integrifolia* L.f. var. *aquilonia* A. S. George. This variety represents the northernmost occurrence of this species, being found in the north Queensland coastal and montane areas from Mt Finnigan National Park near Cooktown to the Paluma Range near Townsville and on Hinchinbrook Island.

Its main difference is in the larger, scattered rather than whorled leaves. The leaves are narrowly obovate-lanceolate, 5–20 cm long by 6–12 mm wide with acute tips.

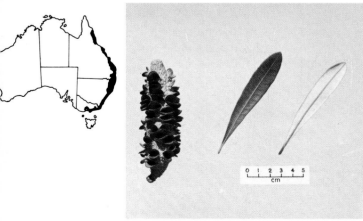

B. *laevigata* Meisn.
subsp. *fuscolutea* A. S. George

DESCRIPTION: A medium-sized, rather open, upright and prickly shrub to about 2 m high, with a spread often greater than its height. It has no lignotuber.

Differing mainly from *B. laevigata* subsp. *laevigata* in its very beautiful rusty brown and yellow inflorescences, the shrub derives its name from this feature, *fuscolutea* meaning 'brownish-yellow'.

Leaves: Two distinct leaf forms occur on this shrub. One is more or less identical to the leaves of *B. laevigata* subsp. *laevigata* — i.e. glabrous, roughly cuneate, usually truncate, and evenly serrated with sharp-pointed teeth cut about one-third of the way to the mid-rib. The leaves are usually 6–15 cm long by 1.5–2 cm wide. In the other form, they are longer and narrower with a distinct acute or narrowly pointed apex.

Flowers: The beautiful globular reddish-yellow inflorescences are the feature of this plant. At the young bud stage they are a dense woolly brown like small pom-poms. As the perianths develop, the limbs become a conspicuous bright yellow, which, with the rusty brown villous perianth tubes, combine to form a magnificent flower about 8–10 cm in diameter. The perianth limbs are smooth like the styles and this feature is its main difference from *B. laevigata* subsp. *laevigata*, which has hairy perianth limbs. The flowers open from the bottom of the spike first, the released styles slightly curved or erect with a long, narrow pollen presenter. The flowering period is in summer.

Fruits: Persistent dead floral parts mainly conceal the flattish furry follicles which are packed tightly on a globular fruiting cone of roughly the same dimensions as the flower spikes.

DISTRIBUTION: This species is found in open sand heath, rocky laterite or granite ridges in dry inland areas of the Eyre and Coolgardie districts of Western Australia in the Southern Cross to Frank Hann National Park areas. Rainfall is usually under 400 mm.

CULTIVATION: This shrub adapts well to cultivation in porous, well-drained slightly acid to neutral soils.

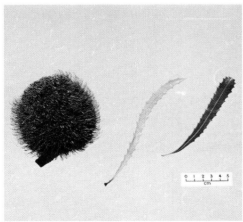

B. laevigata Meisn.
subsp. *laevigata*

DESCRIPTION: An upright, open, but leafy and prickly shrub, usually 2 m or more high, sometimes spreading to a width greater than its height. It has no lignotuber.

The specific name refers to the smooth, glossy leaves, *laevigata* meaning 'smooth'.

Leaves: These are glabrous on both surfaces, roughly cuneate, flat or undulate, usually truncate, and sharply but evenly toothed, the prickly teeth cut about one-third of the way to the mid-rib. They are usually 6–15 cm long by 1.5–2 cm wide, with a prominent mid-rib on both surfaces, the veins reticulate on the under-surface. The young branchlets are commonly clothed with long, soft hairs.

Flowers: 8–10 cm in diameter, the globular flower spikes occur profusely on short branchlets. The perianths are hirsute, the tubes a lemon-yellow, and the limb a woolly grey or sometimes a cream colour. Styles are yellow, smooth, and very straight when released, the pollen presenter narrow and furrowed. The flowering period is spring and summer.

Fruits: The fruiting cones are the same size and shape as the flower spikes, with the dead floral parts persisting and obscuring the follicles. The stiff styles which protrude mainly at right angles to the axis of the spike, and the close-set floral parts, create a dense pincushion or tennis ball effect.

DISTRIBUTION: A shrub found in rocky laterite or light soils in the Ravensthorpe Range and surrounding plains of the Eyre and Stirling districts of Western Australia. Rainfall is 400–600 mm.

CULTIVATION: This shrub adapts well to cultivation, preferring light, well-drained, slightly acid soils, but it succeeds on clay or rocky soils on slopes where the annual rainfall is considerably more than its natural habitat.

B. lanata A. S. George

DESCRIPTION: A spreading shrub without a lignotuber rarely exceeding 1 m tall, with many horizontally, sprawling branches and narrow leaves.

The specific name refers to the woolly (*lanatus*) white floral bracts.

Leaves: Narrowly linear, crowded and scattered, up to 10 cm long and usually under 1 mm wide, the leaves are covered with long, stiff hairs on the under-surface, the margins revolute. Branchlets are woolly hairy. An attractive feature of this shrub is the bright pink new growth.

Flowers: These are usually produced on short lateral branches within the bush, the spike held erect. Each spherical spike 7–10 cm in diameter, comprises many silky hairy perianths, cream to pale brown, opening from the top of the spike first. Styles are purple. It usually flowers between October and January.

Fruits: Resembling a dried version of the flower spike the fruiting cones contain numerous, densely hairy, elliptic follicles and are clothed in persistent dead flowers.

DISTRIBUTION: A Western Australian banksia of localised distribution on heathland adjacent to Eneabba and Mt Lesueur. Soils are deep white sands. Rainfall is 500-600 mm.

CULTIVATION: A fast growing shrub, good as ground cover for light, well-drained soils.

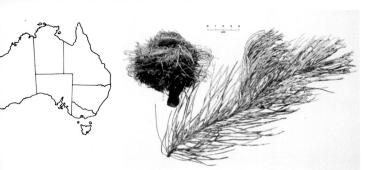

81

B. laricina C. A. Gardn.

ROSE-FRUITED BANKSIA, ROSE BANKSIA

DESCRIPTION: This interesting small to medium-sized shrub is a low, rounded, sometimes straggly, small-leaved bush, 1–1.5 m high, with bark a smoothish grey or grey-brown. It has no lignotuber.

The specific name means 'larch-like' and refers to the conifer-like foliage and fruits which, on a larger scale, bear some resemblance to those of the European Larch Tree. The fruiting cones are its distinguishing feature, being quite unique in their structure.

Leaves: The small, crowded, bright green, narrow-linear leaves are 1–2 cm long, entire, and revolute to the mid-rib, the under-surface white. They are very similar to those of *B. nutans*.

Flowers: The flower spikes which are erect, almost globular, and about 4 cm in diameter, are produced within the foliage, mainly on lateral branches. Although small and not conspicuous, they are individually exquisite when closely examined. The hairy perianths are a dark violet-red, and the thin, wiry, permanently hooked styles are yellow with a tiny, dark brown, conical pollen presenter. Similar to other banksias with styles which remain hooked, these are released from the top of the spike first. Flowering is profuse, from late autumn to mid-winter.

Fruits: The fruiting cones shed the dead flowers soon after fertilisation, leaving smooth green seed follicles which soon turn a brownish or yellowish colour. Their arrangement is a striking feature of the shrub. Thin, wavy, and rounded, they radiate from the slender axis, each follicle like a thick rose petal, the whole effect resembling the rose.

DISTRIBUTION: This rare species is from sandy depressions of the coastal strip on either side of the Moore River just north of Perth, Western Australia. Rainfall is 600–700 mm.

CULTIVATION: This is an easy shrub to establish in light or sandy, slightly acid to neutral soils, flowering well after about three years from planting out.

B. lemanniana Meisn.

LEMANN'S BANKSIA

DESCRIPTION: This species is a large, bushy shrub to 3–4 m tall without a lignotuber. Sometimes dense and spreading, it often grows upright and more open where it competes with other taller plants. It is closely related to Caley's Banksia (*B. caleyi*).

The specific name honours Charles Lemann, a nineteenth-century English botanist.

Leaves: Roughly cuneate to obovate in shape with truncate or retuse apexes, the rigid, slightly wavy leaves are 5–10 cm long by 1.5–4 cm wide. The regular, prickly, saw-toothed margins are divided about a quarter way to the mid-rib. New growth is softly hairy, a brownish-green or rust colour.

Flowers: The profuse flower spikes are 10–16 cm long by 8–12 cm in diameter, ovoid to almost globular, deflexed, yellow or yellow-green in colour. They mainly appear on short branchlets hanging down rather like lighted lanterns set within the foliage. Perianths and styles are glabrous, the styles finally straight after being released. The flowering period is generally spring to early summer.

Fruits: These are large and pendent, with very prominent, almost globular or egg-shaped, furry follicles which protrude about 2 cm from the spike. The dead flowers remain for a long period, the very straight, stiff, grey styles prominent.

DISTRIBUTION: Lemann's Banksia is from the Eyre district of Western Australia's south coast, where it can be seen growing abundantly in the gravelly laterite soils of Mt Desmond near Ravensthorpe and in low heathland near Hopetoun and the Barren Range. Soils can be sand, loam, or clay, pH about neutral. Rainfall is 500–600 mm.

CULTIVATION: This is a reasonably easy species to grow where drainage is good. It makes rapid growth and forms an excellent screening or windbreak shrub with very ornamental flowers.

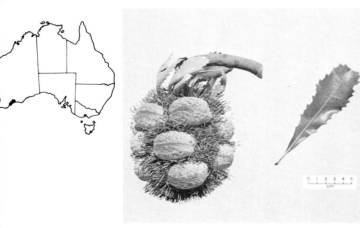

B. leptophylla A. S. George
var. *leptophylla*

DESCRIPTION: A much branched shrub to 2 m high but spreading to 3 m, without a lignotuber and with narrow, pine-like foliage (was once referred to as *B. pinifolia*).

The specific name refers to the slender leaves (from the Greek).

Leaves: These are scattered, narrowly linear, acute, 4–10 cm long by 1–1.5 mm wide. They are hirsute becoming glabrous above, with revolute margins and a woolly under-surface.

Flowers: Spherical to ovoid spikes, 7–12 cm wide, are produced on short lateral branches, a bright golden-yellow to brownish in colour, the styles yellow to purplish, opening from the top of the spike first. It flowers from November to May.

Fruits: Resembling dried versions of the flower spike, the fruiting spikes produce many closely packed, hairy follicles hidden among the persistent old flowers, becoming glabrous when exposed.

DISTRIBUTION: In Western Australia, mainly on inland sand heaths and shrubland, from Tathra National Park near Eneabba south to Mogumber, although this variety was photographed by the authors close to Jurien Bay. Rainfall is 350–700 mm.

B. leptophylla* var. *melletica A. S. George. This variety, first named in 1987, differs from the preceding in its smaller flowers and inflorescences and later flowering period (April–July).

It is generally found nearer the coast (mainly within 30 km) in sandy soils from Kalbarri to Guilderton.

CULTIVATION: Fast growing spreading shrubs for a well-drained light soil in an open situation.

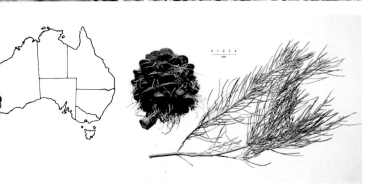

B. lindleyana Meisn.

PORCUPINE BANKSIA

DESCRIPTION: A medium to large, free flowering, open branched, rather twisted shrub, 2–3 m high by a slightly greater width. The lower branches are inclined to be bare of leaves and covered with flaky, grey bark, while the young branchlets and leaves are woolly, grey-green, and give a hoary look to the plant. It has a lignotuber.

The specific name honours John Lindley, an English botanist of the nineteenth century.

Leaves: The leaves are not unlike those of *B. attenuata*, but are inclined to taper much more narrowly at the apex with the greatest width nearer the centre of the leaf. Shallowly and evenly serrated, they are 8–25 cm long by usually under 1 cm wide, linear-lanceolate tapering to a short petiole. The mid-rib is prominent and the margins slightly recurved.

Flowers: Freely produced throughout the shrub, the large, ovoid, erect flower spikes are a lovely pure yellow in colour, usually 10–15 cm long by 7–10 cm in diameter. Both the perianths and styles are glabrous and the prominent styles are very straight and rigid when released from the bottom of the spike first. The pollen presenter is long, narrow, and furrowed. The flowering period is in late summer and autumn.

Fruits: Large, ovoid, fruiting cones are roughly the same size as the inflorescences. The dead floral parts, particularly the conspicuous, stiffly projecting styles, largely obscure the fairly prominent, densely furry follicles.

DISTRIBUTION: This rare species of Western Australian sand heaths is found mainly in the area from Binnu to Kalbarri National Park, often in association with *B. sceptrum*, although it also occurs further north in deep sands towards Shark Bay. Rainfall is 300–350 mm.

CULTIVATION: Porcupine Banksia is a rapid grower in cultivation if given an acid to neutral, sandy soil and an open situation.

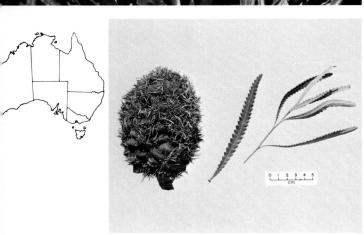

89

B. *littoralis* R. Br.

SWAMP BANKSIA

DESCRIPTION: Usually a medium-sized, thick-trunked, sometimes straggly tree up to 8 m or more high, with a spreading, slightly drooping canopy of branches, and dull grey, rough bark, but grey tomentose on the younger branchlets. It has a lignotuber and after fire usually sprouts from the trunk and branches.

The specific name means 'close to the sea', referring to the tree's coastal habitat, although it also frequently occurs further inland.

Leaves: The long, linear, soft leaves are 8–30 cm long by 4–6 mm wide, scattered, or irregularly whorled, and serrated with a few small soft teeth, usually more frequent near the apex. The margins are recurved and the under-surface is hoary-tomentose or felted white.

Flowers: Erect, cylindrical or oblong spikes, usually under 15 cm long by 4–7 cm in diameter, are produced in the forks between branchlets. Both perianths and styles are yellow, the perianths arranged in vertical rows with each pair of limbs turned in opposite directions. The limbs are silky hairy, the hairs either creamy-white, or brownish, this latter feature giving to the spike a burnished gold appearance at the bud stages. When released, the long smooth styles remain hooked, the pollen presenter small and ovoid. The flowering period is in late summer and winter.

Fruits: The long fruiting cones arise from many small, flat, sharp-edged follicles which protrude prominently from the greyish tomentose rachis, the dead flowers soon falling.

DISTRIBUTION: Although recorded from the Hill River district north of Perth, it is mainly a tree of the coastal plains from near Perth to the Albany area and extending east as far as Bremer Bay in Western Australia. Often grows in low-lying sandy swamps and depressions. Rainfall is 600–1000 mm.

CULTIVATION: Seldom cultivated, it is a tree which could be useful for moist sandy soils, or gardens where assured moisture could be provided, in a temperate climate.

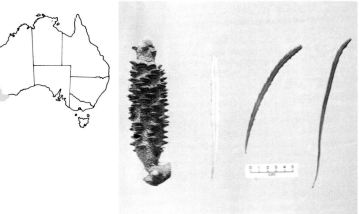

B. lullfitzii C. A. Gardn.

DESCRIPTION: This small shrubby *Banksia* has a number of erect, prickly, rigid branches and flower spikes which are erect and rather hidden among the foliage. It grows only to about 1 m high and has a lignotuber.

The specific name honours Fred Lullfitz, a prominent Western Australian plant collector and nurseryman.

Leaves: These are stiff, erect, long, and narrow, usually 20–50 cm long by about 1 cm or less wide, smooth on both surfaces, the mid-rib prominent and the veins reticulate on the paler green under-surface. They are dentate, the teeth very prickly and regular in shape, but the leaves are sometimes entire over their narrow lower half, tapering to the base. In this and other respects, they resemble the leaves of *B. elderiana*, but they are generally longer and narrower at the very sharp apex and the teeth are more prominent.

Flowers: Set on lateral branches within the foliage, the oblong to ovoid flower spikes, 7–10 cm long by 6–7 cm in diameter, are an attractive buff colour. The perianths, particularly the limb, are very soft and woolly, and the styles smooth. When released, from the bottom of the spike first, the styles curve upwards but do not project far from the opened laminae, the pollen presenter long, narrow, and furrowed. The flowering period is in autumn.

Fruits: The fruiting cones are roughly the same size and shape as the flower spikes with the dead floral parts persistent. Follicles are a flat oval shape and covered with dense woolly hairs.

DISTRIBUTION: A rare plant from the Coolgardie district of Western Australia, this species grows in deep yellow sand in open heathland. It has been found near Southern Cross and in the Ravensthorpe area and probably inhabits sand heath between these two extremes. Rainfall is 250–400 mm, with very dry summers.

CULTIVATION: This species is rare in cultivation but it has grown and flowered at Blackwood in the Adelaide Hills. Soil is a slightly acid sandy loam over clay. Rainfall is about 650 mm.

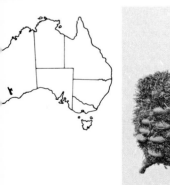

93

B. marginata Cav.

SILVER BANKSIA

DESCRIPTION: Usually a small, much-branched tree, 7–10 m high with rough, grey bark. It also occurs as a low shrub in coastal windswept and rocky, mountain locations. The common name is derived from its leaves which are green above, but white tomentose on the under-surface, giving the whole tree a silvery appearance. Some populations appear to be lignotuberous or resprout from epicormic buds after fire. Some forms show evidence of suckering if roots are disturbed.

Its specific name refers to the distinct leaf margins which appear as a border on the white under-surface.

Leaves: These are mainly narrow, usually under 1 cm wide, linear to oblong-cuneate, 2–10 cm long, with a blunt, usually truncate apex. The margins are recurved, entire, or sometimes serrated with short, distant teeth, the lateral veins on the under-surface are inconspicuous, but the mid-rib is prominent and covered with short, brown hairs, these extending to the young branchlets.

Flowers: The flower spikes are lemon-coloured, 4–10 cm long by 4–6 cm in diameter and cylindrical. The styles finally straighten and subtend a slender, cylindrical, stigmatic end. Perianths are pubescent.

A rewarding sight is when this tree is crowded with flowers at the various stages of development; slender and greenish when in bud, pale yellow at maturity, darkening with age through brown to grey. Finally only the bronze velvety rachis remains. The long flowering period extends from spring to early winter.

Fruits: The mature follicles, which protrude prominently from the spike, are small, flat, and rounded, at first pubescent, but soon becoming smooth. Valves are thin. The dead flowers persist for a considerable time without obscuring the follicles.

DISTRIBUTION: *B. marginata* is found over an extensive range mostly from the wetter parts of South Australia to almost the Queensland border in northern New South Wales. It is common in Tasmania and appears near sea-level on the windswept islands of Bass Strait to the sub-alpine levels of the Alps in Victoria and New South Wales. Its habitat range is generally in areas of cool, moist winters where rainfall exceeds 700 mm, although it also occurs in the Little and Big deserts of Victoria and South Australia (rainfall about 400 mm). Because of its extensive and variable habitat range a number of different forms occur naturally.

CULTIVATION: This tree adapts fairly well to garden conditions where drainage is good. However, its ease of cultivation tends to depend on the source of origin of the seed. For example, one form grows in the Grampian Mountains in Victoria where the soil is very acid (pH 4.5–5) while it also inhabits slightly alkaline soils in parts of South Australia.

B. media R. Br.

GOLDEN STALK, SOUTHERN PLAINS BANKSIA

DESCRIPTION: Well known in cultivation, this is a medium to large shrub without a lignotuber, 2–4 m or more high, dense and leafy, and branching to ground level. The younger branches are covered with dense, minute, whitish hairs which can give the shrub a hoary appearance. In some localities it grows almost to the sea and, under these conditions, will often spread to 4 m or more across while the winds restrict its height to 1 m or less.

The specific name means 'medium' or 'in between'.

Leaves: These are 6–15 cm long by about 2 cm wide on a short leaf stalk, roughly cuneate, undulate to sinuate, the apex more or less truncate, and the margins usually fairly evenly serrated with small, sharp teeth. They are glabrous above but the under-surface is coated with fine yellow-brown hairs which soon wear off, the mid-rib prominent.

Flowers: The spike is cylindrical, 12–20 cm long by 8–10 cm in diameter, terminal, erect, and prominent, a bright creamy-yellow at first, but darkening with age. Flowers are variable, sometimes the hairy perianth tips are a dark brown, this feature lessening the brightness of colour. There is a form which is almost orange. The smooth styles curve upwards when released and the perianths are partly villous, the lower end of the tube being smooth. The main flowering period is February to early spring.

Fruits: The cones are the same size and shape as the flower spikes, the thick, smooth but dimpled, dark brown follicles virtually hidden by the persistent remains of the dead flowers, which turn a bright bronze colour before ageing to grey.

DISTRIBUTION: An inhabitant of Western Australia's south coast between the eastern end of the Stirling Ranges to Israelite Bay, with an outlier near Point Culver at the Great Australian Bight, this species can be found growing almost to the sea as well as inland. It often grows in dense thickets in sand plain communities, but is found on a variety of soils, including crumbly clay and solid coastal limestone. Rainfall is 300–600 mm.

CULTIVATION: *B. media* is one of the easiest banksias to cultivate and one which will tolerate fairly alkaline soils. Light well-drained soils are preferred. Growth is rapid and flowering occurs after two or three years from planting out. An outstanding ornamental shrub.

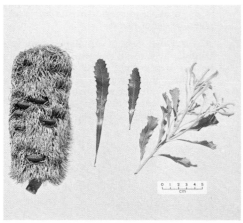

97

B. meisneri Lehm.
var. *meisneri*
MEISNER'S BANKSIA

DESCRIPTION: One of the smaller shrubby banksias with heath-like foliage. This is distinctive and attractive because of the crowded reflexed arrangement of the leaves. Not a common species, it is usually a spreading, somewhat straggly shrub reaching 1–1.5 m high in its native habitat, but will grow larger than this when cultivated. It has no lignotuber.

The specific name honours Carl Meissner, a Swiss botanist.

Leaves: These are small, heath-like, narrow-linear or almost terete, up to 7 mm in length, crowded along the branches either at right angles or more often reflexed, and numerous, soft and not sharply pointed.

Flowers: The small squat flower spikes are seldom more than 4 cm in diameter, more or less cylindrical in shape and are borne on lateral branches. Yellow in colour, they are noted for their gleaming metallic, golden-yellow, smooth styles which remain permanently hooked when released from the top of the spike first. The hairy perianths are less than half the length of the styles and the tiny pollen presenter is dark and rounded. Flowers occur from autumn to spring.

Fruits: The fruiting cones are more or less globular but commonly flat on the top and bottom surfaces, and about 5 cm in diameter. At first a dense woolly white, the flat, deeply embedded follicles wear to a smooth, but wrinkled surface. The dead floral parts are soon shed.

DISTRIBUTION: This is a rare species from the south-central wheat belt and adjacent Darling Ranges of Western Australia. Restricted to near Collie, it extends eastwards to Katanning and south to the Stirling Ranges. Mainly found on sand, it also occurs in shallow clay depressions. Rainfall is 500–900 mm.

CULTIVATION: This shrub grows more robustly in cultivation and responds to light pruning. It flowers prolifically after four or five years, thriving in well-drained sandy soils, with some protection given by other plants.

B. meisneri Lehm. var. ***ascendens*** A. S. George. Scott River Banksia. Even more rare than the preceding, this variety differs in its leaf arrangement, with these being ascending or sometimes spreading and some 8–15 mm long. The varietal name *ascendens* refers to the leaf arrangement.

It occurs in a limited area south-east of Busselton and on the Scott River plains east of Augusta.

99

B. menziesii R. Br.

FIREWOOD BANKSIA, MENZIES' BANKSIA

DESCRIPTION: A tree of crooked and gnarled growth, 8–15 m high, with thick spreading branches at maturity. It has rough, pebbled bark which is thick and woolly on the younger branches. Contains a lignotuber and after fire may shoot from epicormic buds.

The specific name commemorates Archibald Menzies, an eighteenth-century botanist.

Leaves: These are 15–30 cm long by 2·5–4 cm wide, usually slightly wavy, the margins lined with very small, sharply pointed teeth (dentate) in a regular pattern, and the yellow mid-rib prominent. Their under-surface is covered with rusty hairs and marked by numerous parallel transverse veins.

Flowers: Flowering spikes, 10–12 cm long and nearly this width, are cylindrical in bud, at first a velvety silver-grey, then red tipped with silver, before the flowers begin to open and release wiry golden styles. As they open from the bottom of the spike first, the spike becomes acorn-shaped, taking on a wine-red, silver, and gold colour with an arrangement in neat vertical rows.

The perianth tubes, usually red, also occur in yellow and reddish-yellow colour forms. A distinguishing feature is the styles, which are tipped with long, golden, deeply-furrowed pollen presenters.

The flowering period is in autumn and winter.

Fruits: Mature seed cones display a few, prominent, scattered, furry seed follicles protruding from a small but beautifully textured spike. This is regularly patterned and resembles the weave in a grey and brown felted cloth. The seeds are freely released naturally.

DISTRIBUTION: The habitat range extends from the Pinjarra district south of Perth to Kalbarri in the north, and inland on the northern sand heaths of the Avon district of Western Australia. Rainfall is 300–900 mm.

CULTIVATION: The seeds are relatively easy to extract, they germinate well, and young seedlings are not difficult to raise. However, away from its native State this has not been an easy species to grow, although it does well on deep sand (pH 6·5) in the south-east of South Australia and adjacent to Happy Valley Reservoir near Adelaide.

0 1 2 3 4 5
cm

101

B. micrantha A. S. George

DESCRIPTION: A low, sprawling shrub less than 1 m in height. A unique feature in this group of banksias (Abietinae) is the branches which first appear below the ground. The shrub, which has a ligno-tuber, is often twice as wide as its height. The smaller branchlets are silky hairy (pubescent) and the foliage bright green and needle-like. Confusion has been experienced in separating this species from *B. sphaerocarpa* var. *sphaerocarpa* where they grow together in the sand heaths of the Eneabba and Badgingarra areas.

The specific name refers to the small flowers.

Leaves: These are scattered, linear and sharply-pointed, 1–3 cm long by 1–1.5 mm wide, with revolute margins. They are mainly glabrous above but woolly hairy below (tomentose).

Flowers: Small, globular inflorescences are produced terminally or on lateral branches. These are greenish in bud but mature to yellow or a purplish-yellow due to the smooth styles. Perianths are closely pubescent outside and inside while the limbs are mostly glabrous. Glabrous limbs are the main feature that distinguishes this species from *B. sphaerocarpa* var. *sphaerocarpa* where the limbs are hairy.

The flowering period is summer through to autumn.

Fruits: These are more or less the same shape and size as the inflorescences, supporting large and prominent ovate-elliptic follicles, at first silky hairy but becoming glabrous as they age. The dead flowers remain on the spike indefinitely, a feature that assists in distinguishing this species from *B. incana* where the flowers fall rapidly, other features of the two species being similar.

DISTRIBUTION: A shrub of low heathland in shallow sand over laterite, rainfall about 600 mm. It is of restricted distribution in the Eneabba and Badgingarra areas of Western Australia.

CULTIVATION: This slow-growing shrub prefers a sunny position in well-drained sandy or gravelly soil. Successful plants are growing under these conditions at Victor Harbor and Happy Valley, South Australia.

B. nutans R. Br.
var. *nutans*
NODDING BANKSIA

DESCRIPTION: One of the small, ground-hugging banksias with tiny, linear leaves and inconspicuous flower spikes. It usually grows to about 1 m high with several, thin, spreading branches, its spread often more than its height. It has no lignotuber.

The specific name *nutans* means 'nodding' and refers to the deflexed direction of the small, pendent flower spikes on slender, decurved branchlets.

Leaves: These are very small, glabrous, narrow-linear, usually less than 1 mm wide with the margins rolled back to the mid-rib, and up to about 2 cm in length but usually less. The apex of each leaf is aristate to acute.

Flowers: Ovoid to cylindrical, the small, reflexed flower spikes are approximately 6–8 cm long by 5–6 cm in diameter. Purplish-brown at maturity, the young spikes are cream, tinged pink, due to the hairy perianth tubes and limbs. Perianth tubes are more than half the length of the styles. The flowers open from the base of the spike first, releasing smooth, yellow styles with a small, conical pollen presenter, the styles remaining permanently hooked. Flowers are strongly onion-scented.

The main flowering period is in summer.

Fruits: The fruiting cones are mainly larger than the flower spikes, the dead flowers remaining, but these are mostly obscured by large, closely packed, very wide follicles. These are a distinctive feature, being wedge-shaped tapering inwards, with a very wrinkled but glabrous texture. They are bright green at first but age to grey.

DISTRIBUTION: This species is from the Stirling and Eyre districts of Western Australia. It extends from the Stirling Ranges to Israelite Bay, usually on sandy loams. Rainfall is 350–500 mm.

B. nutans R. Br. var. ***cernuella*** A. S. George. This variety differs in its smaller flowering spikes and fruits, the follicles being flattened but convex and only slightly wrinkled. The flowering period is later than var. *nutans*, being mid-summer to autumn.

Its distribution is also further west extending from west of Katanning eastwards almost to the Fitzgerald River National Park.

CULTIVATION: Both varieties are best suited to sandy soils, which are slightly acid (pH 6.5), and a sunny open position.

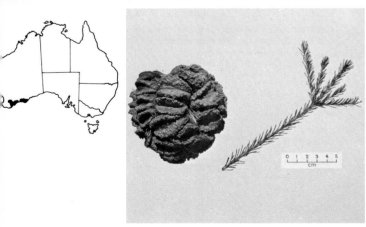

B. oblongifolia Cav.
var. *oblongifolia*

DESCRIPTION: This is a low, straggly or compact shrub usually not more than 1 m high with many stems arising from a lignotuber, its spread often greater than its height.

The specific name refers to the shape of the leaves.

Leaves: The leathery leaves are irregularly toothed (serrate) or almost entire, mainly less than 11 cm long, by about 15–25 mm wide, elliptical-oblong to obovate in shape, white and downy on the under-surface, being clothed with a conspicuous, dense, rusty-red tomentum. The young shoots and branchlets are also covered with dense rusty hairs enhancing the overall appearance of the plant. Distinct parallel primary veins feature on the under-surface.

Flowers: When fully out the cylindrical flower spikes are lemon in colour, up to 10 cm long by 5–6 cm in diameter. At the bud stages, however, they are usually bluish-green due to the villous perianths. The smooth yellow styles, which are released from the bottom of the spike first, are spreading, or lightly reflexed, and tipped with a small brown pollen presenter.

The main flowering period occurs in autumn and early winter.

Fruits: Cylindrical fruiting cones contain deeply embedded furry seed follicles in parallel rows, the dead flowers soon being shed.

DISTRIBUTION: A species from the east coast regions of New South Wales and Queensland, abundant in sandy swamp margins near the coast, extending from Wollongong, south of Sydney, northwards to Bundaberg and Fraser Island in Queensland. Rainfall is 700–1300 mm and occurs throughout the year.

B. oblongifolia Cav. var. **minor** (Maiden and Camfield) Conran and Clifford. This variety is a taller, more erect shrub 1–3.5 mm high, with fewer basal stems arising from its lignotuber and generally longer leaves, up to 14 cm long. It is mainly found at higher levels than the preceding variety, in heath understorey to open forest on sandstone, granite, or sandy-clay ridges. It occurs over a similar range as var. *oblongifolia* but extends further north and inland to the Blackdown Tableland in Queensland.

CULTIVATION: This species grows well on moist acid, sandy soils, but is unknown by the authors under other conditions.

B. occidentalis R. Br.
subsp. *occidentalis*

WATER BUSH, RED SWAMP BANKSIA

DESCRIPTION: Normally a large, erect, dense foliaged shrub, but sometimes a small tree to 7 m high, with slender leaves and smoothish brown-grey bark. Bark on the young branchlets is smooth and bright red or orange. It bears similarities to certain eastern species — e.g. *B. spinulosa*, and *B. ericifolia*. It has no ligno-tuber.

The specific name means 'western' and obviously refers to its Western Australian habitat, although there are sixty other Western Australian *Banksia* species.

Leaves: These are narrow-linear, 5–15 cm long by 2–3 mm wide, smooth, dull green above with a white reverse, the margins revolute. They are mainly entire, with a few fine teeth near the notched ends, but sometimes with small teeth (denticulate) spaced irregularly along the full length of the leaf. The leaves are borne in regular whorls around the branches.

Flowers: Attractive, ruby-red cylindrical spikes, 10–15 cm long by about 6–9 cm in diameter, are borne in great numbers. The smooth perianths are honey-yellow or cream and the styles, which remain permanently hooked after the perianth has opened, a bright crimson.

The flowering period is in summer and early autumn.

Fruits: Narrowly cylindrical, the fruiting spikes retain the dead flowers for a considerable time. These usually hide the follicles which are thin, rounded and often crowded thickly on the spike.

DISTRIBUTION: This species is practically always found in wet situations — swampy, peaty sands near the coast from Augusta to Cape Arid in Western Australia. Rainfall is 600–800 mm.

CULTIVATION: One of the easier banksias to cultivate, it grows vigorously in the garden, particularly if given ample water. However, light, neutral to slightly acid soils are preferred. This is an ornamental species well-suited to many garden conditions.

B. occidentalis R. Br. subsp.***formosa*** Hopper. This shrub differs from the former in its lower-growing (to 2 m tall), compact habit, shorter, wider leaves and profuse flowering over the whole canopy of the bush. It is known from the Black Point Peninsula, approximately 40 km east of Augusta, and near Mutton Bird Island, just west of Albany, Western Australia. An ideal garden shrub.

B. oligantha A. S. George

DESCRIPTION: A relatively slender shrub to 3 m high with few main stems and without a lignotuber. The bark on the lower part of the trunk is rough and the branchlets hairy but becoming glabrous.

This is a very rare shrub, first collected in 1984 (by Ken Wallace) and only named in 1987. It is closely related to *B. cuneata,* another endangered species, and *B. ilicifolia.*

The specific name (from the Greek) refers to the few-flowered inflorescences, one of the features by which it differs from *B. cuneata* and *B. ilicifolia.*

Leaves: The very concave, obovate, prickly-toothed leaves are normally 1.5 to 3.5 cm long and up to 2 cm wide, obtuse with a sharp mucro, and deep shining green on the upper surface (compare with the dull green leaves of *B. cuneata*).

Flowers: The inflorescence is a terminal, few-flowered, rounded head, 2.5–3 cm across, creamy-yellow to the glance, although the closely pubescent perianths are reddish over their lower half, grading to cream and pale yellow at the limb. Styles are cream.

Flowering occurs in mid to late spring.

Fruits: These appear as a single, or small cluster of ovoid, curved follicles, each follicle up to 2 cm long by nearly 1 cm wide, and closely tomentose on the outer surface. They shed their seed naturally without heat from fires, a feature shared with *B. ilicifolia* but not *B. cuneata.*

DISTRIBUTION: Only known from a small nature reserve 28 km north-west of Wagin in Western Australia's wheatbelt, growing in sandy soil among other tall shrubs. Rainfall is 450–500 mm.

CULTIVATION: Unknown in cultivation (1988).

B. oreophila A. S. George

WESTERN MOUNTAIN BANKSIA

DESCRIPTION: A relative of the Oak-leaved Banksia (*B. quercifolia*), Western Mountain Banksia is similar in many respects, its main differences being in the leaves which are usually entire, its grey-mauve flowers and larger follicles. It was previously named *B. quercifolia* var. *integrifolia*. It is an erect, sometimes spreading, densely branched shrub, 2 m or more high, with smoothish, grey-brown bark. A feature is the distinct blue colour of the leaves. It has no lignotuber.

The specific name means 'mountain loving', referring to the shrub's habitat.

Leaves: These are irregularly wedge-shaped with entire margins, or sometimes with a few irregular, sharp-pointed teeth. They are glabrous, generally slightly narrower than the leaves of *B. quercifolia*, usually about 2 cm wide by 5–12 cm long, and a blue-green in colour, the margins flat or undulate.

Flowers: The cylindrical flower spikes closely resemble those of *B. quercifolia*, but are often slightly larger (6–15 cm long by 4–7 cm in diameter) and mature to a grey or grey-mauve colour. In all other respects they are identical — the individual flowers arranged in neat vertical rows, awn-like appendages attached to each silky, hairy perianth, and smooth, yellow styles mainly hidden by the floral appendages.

The flowering period is from late summer to winter.

Fruits: The mature fruiting cones are slightly larger than the flower spikes, due to the follicles which are smooth, large and rounded, rather like small walnuts. The dead flowers are persistent.

DISTRIBUTION: This shrub is confined to rocky (often quartzite) soils, either on mountain slopes or at their base in dense scrub. It grows near the summit of some of the high peaks of the Stirling Ranges, a feature from which it derives its common name, and is also found on the Barrens Range in the Fitzgerald River National Park. Rainfall is 500–600 mm.

CULTIVATION: This is a tough, hardy species in cultivation, but it requires good drainage when compared with *B. quercifolia*, which can be grown in swampy ground.

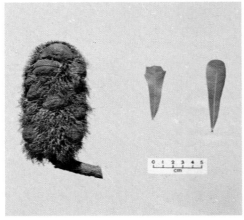

B. ornata F. Muell. ex Meisn.

DESERT BANKSIA

DESCRIPTION: A bushy shrub 1–3 m high with rough, grey bark and handsome foliage. This species is generally found growing in thickets where the soil is deep and sandy. It is noted for the colour variations which occur naturally in its flowers. It has no lignotuber.

The specific name refers to its ornamental appearance, particularly the flowers.

Leaves: These are 5–8 cm long by 2–3 cm broad, regularly serrated, oblong-cuneate in shape and truncate or obtuse at the tips. Mature leaves are rigid, glabrous, the margins flat or undulating. The oblique lateral nerves and mid-rib are prominently displayed on the under-surface.

Young leaves are red-coloured, soft, and hairy, and enhance the foliage appeal of this plant.

Flowers: The flower spikes are 5–14 cm long, often as broad as their length in the shorter spikes. Their shape is ovoid or oblong, the perianths soft and hairy. Colours range from grey and yellow (common), to a beautiful velvety bronze, with many colour variations between these two extremes. The pollen presenter on the style is ovoid and furrowed, a dark, purplish-red in the common form. The flowers open from the bottom of the spike first.

The flowering period is in autumn and winter.

Fruits: These are ovoid or cylindrical, the densely furry seed follicles mainly hidden by the withered floral parts which persist indefinitely on the cone.

DISTRIBUTION: This species occurs in areas of deep sandy soils in many parts of South Australia and in western Victoria. These include the Mt Lofty Ranges, particularly the Fleurieu Peninsula, Kangaroo Island, the Marble Range on Eyre Peninsula, the southeast, and the Ninety-Mile Desert including the Big Desert in Victoria. Rainfall is 400–700 mm.

CULTIVATION: A relatively easy species to grow on sandy well-drained, neutral to slightly acid soils, but does not adapt readily to the heavier soil types.

B. paludosa R. Br.

MARSH BANKSIA, SWAMP BANKSIA

DESCRIPTION: A low shrubby species with lignotuber, seldom more than 1 m high. Although not spectacular, it is attractive because of its foliage which is not unlike a small bush version of the Coast Banksia (*B. integrifolia*).

Its specific and common name refers to a boggy or marshy habitat. This is partly misleading because the plant grows in rocky sandstones on high rainfall mountain plateaus, near the coast and near swamps.

Leaves: In their whorled arrangement (usually three or four together) and shape, the variable leaves resemble those of *B. integrifolia*. Oblanceolate to narrowly elliptic, they are 4–10 cm long by 1–2 cm wide, whitish tomentose to smooth on the undersurface (sometimes with soft brown hairs mainly along the mid-rib), almost entire, or quite markedly toothed, particularly near the upper part, the margins very recurved. They point upwards at an angle of about forty-five degrees, while the veins are distinctly oblique and curve upwards (cf. the veins of *B. integrifolia* which are almost transverse and comparatively straight). The young branches are almost glabrous, as they are coated with a few brownish hairs.

Flowers: The flower spikes are narrow and generally quite small (5–10 cm long by 3–4 cm in diameter). Although not prominently displayed, at the late bud stage in particular, they have a look of burnished gold which, when combined with the plant's smooth handsome foliage, is most attractive. The pale yellow, short, smooth styles, which open from the bottom of the spike first, are finally quite straight and strictly at right angles to the axis of the spike, the pollen presenter small and brown. Perianths are brownish and silky hairy.

The flowering period is in late autumn and winter.

Fruits: These bear no resemblance to those of *B. integrifolia*. The cones are narrow-oblong, the follicles protruding only slightly. Follicles are flattish-ovoid with a prominent suture and slightly hairy, the dead flowers persistent for some time.

DISTRIBUTION: This is a comparatively rare species from wet sandstone soils of the east coast of New South Wales. It occurs in two disjunct populations, one on the coastal strip and adjacent mountains from the Lithgow area south almost to Batemans Bay and the other on the coastal strip from the Eden area south to the Victorian border.

CULTIVATION: This species should succeed in wet, elevated locations on porous soils.

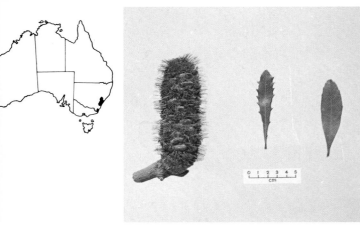

117

B. petiolaris F. Muell.

DESCRIPTION: Another of the prostrate western banksias with spreading horizontal branches on the surface or just covered, and erect leaves and flower spikes. It is without a lignotuber.

The specific name refers to the leaf stalks or petioles, which are quite pronounced in this species.

Leaves: The arrangement of the leaves is more or less vertically erect along the branches, but never around the flower spikes. Dentate, undulate to sinuate, the leaves, 20–40 cm long, tend to be narrower (2–5 cm) with more regular teeth. The long thin leaf-stalks curl around the branches and are arranged spirally on the branches (usually just below the ground).

The mid-rib, oblique and parallel transverse veins are conspicuous. Both surfaces are usually coated with dense woolly hairs and the young growth is grey and softly hairy.

Flowers: Erect at the ends of the leafy stems, the inflorescences are 10–20 cm long by 5–7 cm in diameter, cylindrical, with the individual flowers tightly packed, yellow and brownish-pink in colour. When released, the smooth yellow styles curve upwards, the pollen presenter small and dark in colour. The perianths are densely hairy.

The flowering period is in spring and summer.

Fruits: These are similar in shape and size to the flower spikes, the dead floral parts persistent. Seed follicles are prominent, densely furry, with a protruding suture.

DISTRIBUTION: *B. petiolaris* is from the Eyre district of Western Australia, mainly in sand heath, extending from the Munglinup area east to Israelite Bay. Rainfall is 350–400 mm.

CULTIVATION: This species is easily cultivated in sandy soils which are slightly acid to neutral. It is an excellent rock garden plant.

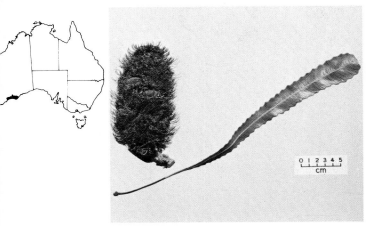

B. pilostylis C. A. Gardn.

DESCRIPTION: This shrub is very similar in appearance to *B. media*. It is a well-branched, dense, bushy shrub, 2–3 m high with a similar spread, the young growth a bright bronze-green or golden-brown colour, due to soft rusty hairs on both surfaces of the leaves. It has no lignotuber.

The specific name refers to the soft, hairy styles of the flowers. *Leaves:* The mature deep green leaves are normally 12–20 cm long by about 2 cm wide, but they can be much longer. They are covered with very short fine hairs on the upper surface and are furry on the reverse side. They are dentate with short, sharp teeth set at fairly regular but long intervals. Cuneate, truncate or retuse, the mid-rib is prominent on the under-surface, and the margins are revolute. Young growth takes on an attractive golden-brown colour and a velvety texture.

Flowers: Flower spikes are ovoid to oblong, 7–15 cm long by 5–8 cm in diameter, yellow to yellowish-green in colour. The spikes have a soft, woolly look prior to the flowers opening, due to the softly hairy covering on all the floral parts — perianths and styles. The styles when finally released are straight or slightly curved with a brownish pollen presenter.

Flowering mainly occurs from late spring to early autumn. *Fruits:* These are ovoid, similar in size to the flower spikes, with the dead flowers persisting as a dense, woolly, grey covering partly obscuring the seed follicles. The smooth brown follicles are dimpled or warted and protrude prominently from the spike.

DISTRIBUTION: This species grows in dense thickets in the deep white or yellow sands of the Eyre district of Western Australia. It extends from the Munglinup area eastwards to the Cape Arid National Park, being common adjacent to the Young River and the area north and north-east of Esperance. Rainfall 300–400 mm.

CULTIVATION: This shrub requires a well-drained soil, open, sunny situation in a fairly dry climate, and little attention once established. Soils pH 6 to pH 7.5 are best.

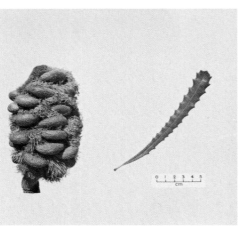

B. *plagiocarpa* A. S. George

DALLACHY'S BANKSIA

DESCRIPTION: A shrub or small tree to 5 m with a short trunk and spreading canopy. Bark is a corky grey-brown, fissured, and the smaller branchlets are woolly and rusty brown in colour. It probably has no lignotuber and there is evidence that after fire, sprouts come from epicormic buds.

The specific name is derived from the Greek and refers to the oblique, upturned fruit follicles.

Leaves: These are narrowly lanceolate to narrowly oblanceolate, 8–20 cm long by 6–17 mm wide, with recurved margins and a prominent rusty hairy central vein on the reverse or underside which contrasts with the white tomentum of the top side of the leaf. They are entire or on some leaves toothed (obtusely serrate). New growth is a velvety red or rust colour.

Flowers: The cylindrical inflorescences up to 14 cm long and 5–6 cm wide are greenish-blue to greyish-green in bud but becoming a yellowish-green as the smooth pale yellow styles open from the bottom of the spike first. Perianths are silky hairy on the outside but smooth inside.

Fruits: The old flowers soon fall to leave a large cylindrical spike with upturned, narrowly elliptic follicles which are covered in a rusty tomentum ageing to grey.

DISTRIBUTION: A Queensland species of restricted distribution in sandy or clay-loam on rocky granite slopes in shrubland. It is restricted to Hinchinbrook Island off the coast between Cardwell and Ingham and the adjacent mainland. Rainfall is 2400 mm annually.

CULTIVATION: Not known by the authors but obviously a species requiring a high rainfall, tropical or subtropical climate and well-drained soil.

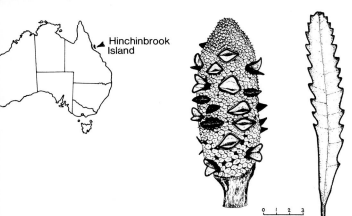

Hinchinbrook Island

123

B. praemorsa Andrews

CUT-LEAF BANKSIA

DESCRIPTION: A medium to large shrub, 2–4 m high, which is usually straggly in its windswept natural habitat but has a very distinct upright habit when cultivated. The many thin leafy branches have smoothish grey-green bark and they are vertically erect. It has no lignotuber.

The specific name means 'dissected' and refers to the blunt or truncated leaves.

Leaves: The short, truncate leaves are 2–5 cm long by 1–2 cm wide, regularly serrated with small sharp teeth cut about one-quarter of the way to the mid-rib. They are oblong-cuneate or obovate in shape and glabrous on both surfaces. The young leaves are golden-brown and soft, enhancing the shrub's appearance when it develops new growth.

Flowers: Long and cylindrical, the spikes are large, up to 30 cm or more long by 8–10 cm in diameter, unique in their colour arrangement. Smooth perianth tubes, limbs, and styles combine to form changing colour patterns according to the light effect. Perianth tubes are wine-red, or dusky purple, grading to yellow near the base, the limbs grey-green, or yellowish, and the styles yellow with a tiny pollen presenter. The styles are short and straight when released, the flowers opening from the bottom of the spike first.

The flowering period is spring.

Fruits: The fruiting cones are large, roughly the same size and shape as the flower spikes with a tangled mass of dead flowers persisting for a long period and completely obscuring the follicles. When exposed, the follicles are smooth and dimpled, rather similar to the follicles of *B. media* and *B. epica*.

DISTRIBUTION: This is a restricted species from the coastal areas of Torbay near Albany, east to near Cape Riche and always within 2 km of the coast, in the Stirling district of Western Australia. Where it is found, however, it is often locally abundant. Rainfall is 700–800 mm.

CULTIVATION: Cut-leaf Banksia is not well known in cultivation but very successfully grown in perfectly drained sandy loam over limestone, soil pH about neutral, and rainfall 700 mm. Because of its natural habitat it could be successful in coastal locations.

125

B. prionotes Lindl.

ORANGE BANKSIA, ACORN BANKSIA

DESCRIPTION: A most beautiful tree *Banksia*, 6–10 m high, often regular and upright in shape with soft, hoary, grey-white bark, but darker grey and marbled on the old limbs, with handsome foliage and brilliant flowers. The new leaves, flower buds, and bark on the younger branches are soft and woolly white. It is without a lignotuber.

The specific name is Latin for 'saw-like', referring to the saw-toothed leaf margins.

Leaves: These are glabrous, flat or undulate, long and linear, 10–30 cm long by 1·5–2·5 cm wide, and divided, about halfway to the mid-rib in the narrower leaf forms but less in others, into evenly spaced triangular lobes. The mid-rib is prominent on both surfaces, the venation on the under-surface consisting of numerous, fine, secondary veins converging to the apex of each lobe.

Flowers: Extremely ornamental, the conspicuous, erect, terminal flower spikes owe their acorn-like appearance to the rigid, bright orange styles, which open from the bottom of the spike first, and the woolly, white perianth limbs of the unopened flowers. In bud the entire spikes are a woolly white and are almost as beautiful as when the flowers open. The spikes are 10–15 cm long by about 8 cm in diameter. Finally straight and erect, but incurved at the base, the styles are tipped by a narrow, furrowed, fusiform pollen presenter. Perianth tubes and limbs are both villous.

Flowers mainly occur in autumn.

Fruits: The fruiting cones are quite small, ovoid, and quickly shed the dead flowers, leaving the small, furry follicles well-embedded in the spike. Very often the seed is ejected as soon as it ripens.

DISTRIBUTION: This is a widely-distributed species, extending from the King George Sound area near Albany to the Shark Bay area in Western Australia. It occurs on finely textured sandy soils with rainfall of 300–900 mm.

CULTIVATION: *B. prionotes* has adapted well to cultivation and has been successfully grown on well-drained limestone soils as well as acid sands.

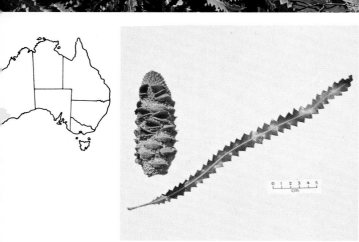

127

B. pulchella R. Br.

TEASEL BANKSIA

DESCRIPTION: This dense, but spreading, low shrub grows to 1 m high, has heath-like foliage and numerous small, erect flowers. Its flower spikes and fruits bear a resemblance to those of *B. meisneri*. It has no lignotuber.

The specific name means 'beautiful', although in the writers' opinion it is not one of the most beautiful banksias.

Leaves: These are 1–1.5 cm long, narrow-linear, the margins revolute to the mid-rib, and the apex not sharply pointed. They are incurved or erect, and crowded along the thin branches. Leaves can be smooth or hairy.

Flowers: The small, straw-yellow, globular flower spikes, about 4 cm in diameter, are borne in great numbers. Perianths are villous and less than half the length of the released styles. The flowers open from the top of the spike first, the smooth styles remaining permanently hooked with a tiny rounded pollen presenter.

In bud the spikes are cone-like and an attractive salmon-pink colour.

The flowering period is summer through to early spring.

Fruits: Irregularly rounded, the nut-like fruiting cones are small, about 3–4 cm in diameter, with smooth flat follicles. Well embedded in the rachis of similar colour and texture they are barely distinguishable from them. The dead flowers fall quickly.

DISTRIBUTION: A shrub of the sand heaths of the Eyre district of Western Australia, *B. pulchella* extends from Fitzgerald River National Park east to Israelite Bay. It is sometimes subjected to damp, almost swampy conditions after heavy rains. Rainfall is 350–500 mm.

CULTIVATION: This shrub requires well-drained, light, slightly acid soils in a temperate climate. Rarely exceeding dwarf shrub proportions the Teasel Banksia is useful as a foreground or rock-garden ground cover plant.

B. quercifolia R. Br.

OAK-LEAVED BANKSIA

DESCRIPTION: An upright or spreading, many-stemmed and dense shrub to 3 m high by about the same width. The bark is smoothish, brown to grey-brown, and although the numerous flowers are not conspicuous they add interest to a shrub worth growing for its attractive foliage. It has no lignotuber.

The specific name refers to the coarsely toothed, oak-like leaves.

Leaves: These are 5–12 cm long by 2–4 cm wide, rigid, flat or undulate, cuneate with long irregular serrations, the teeth sharply-pointed, a dull grey-green and smooth on both surfaces.

Flowers: Flower spikes are small, cylindrical, 5–10 cm long by 4–6 cm in diameter. Grey-brown in bud, they mature to a tan or bronze colour, the flowers being set in neat vertical rows. An unusual feature is the slender, reflexed points which protrude from each individual flower (awn-like appendages attached to each silky, hairy perianth similar to those of *B. baueri*). Styles are smooth and yellow but are mainly hidden by the floral appendages.

The flowering period is late summer to winter.

Fruits: The cones are roughly the same shape and size as the flower spikes with flat, prominent follicles and the dead floral parts are quite persistent.

DISTRIBUTION: Oak-leaved Banksia is a species from Windy Harbour east to Cheyne Beach, in the Stirling and Warren districts of Western Australia where it mainly inhabits sandy, peaty swamps or low-lying country, either near the coast or further inland. Rainfall is 800–900 mm.

CULTIVATION: This species is one of the hardiest banksias, and is suited to light, or fairly heavy, acid soils in full sun or semi-shade. It will stand poor drainage.

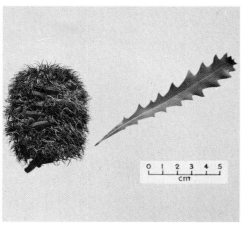

B. repens Labill.

CREEPING BANKSIA

DESCRIPTION: A prostrate species with lignotuber, creeping underground branches and erect, handsome leaves and flower spikes.

The specific name means 'creeping' and refers to the plant's habit.

Leaves: These are scattered and erect, 20–50 cm long, up to 18 cm wide, deeply lobed virtually to the rigid and prominent mid-rib. The lobes are irregular, cuneate to triangular with blunt teeth. The leaves are tomentose when young but become glabrous as they age.

Flowers: Flower spikes are erect at the ends of the creeping branches usually away from the leaves. Perianths are cream with a pink limb, hirsute on the outside but smooth inside. Styles are cream or pale pink, smooth and opening from the bottom of the spike first.

Flowering period is usually October-November.

Fruits: Fruiting cones are similar in size and shape to the flower spikes and the dead floral parts persist. Follicles are prominent, flat and densely furry (tomentose).

DISTRIBUTION: A plant of the sand heaths near the south coast of Western Australia from the Stirling Ranges to Israelite Bay. It sometimes occurs in coastal dunes. Annual rainfall is 350–600 mm.

CULTIVATION: An adaptable, but slow growing plant which succeeds if given 40–50 cm of sandy topsoil of neutral to slightly acid reaction. Prefers a sunny aspect but will tolerate dappled shade.

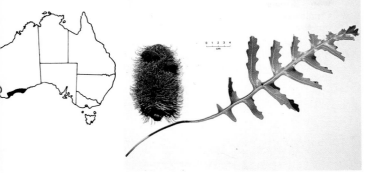

B. robur Cav.

SWAMP BANKSIA, BROAD-LEAVED BANKSIA

DESCRIPTION: A distinctive, easily-recognised species because of its very large, glossy leaves. Usually a woody shrub no more than 2 m high, it sometimes grows taller with a few slender branches when shaded or crowded out by other plants. The bark on the mature limbs is a downy grey, but densely hairy and a rusty-brown on the younger branches. It has a lignotuber.

The specific name is derived from the large, firm, oak-like leaves, *robur* meaning an oak tree, and also meaning strength or firmness. *Leaves:* Exceptionally large by eastern *Banksia* standards, the stiff leaves grow up to 30 cm in length and up to 10 cm wide. These are obovate-oblong in shape, with irregular, shallow serrations along the wavy margins, each tooth tipped with a sharp spine. They are a dark, glossy green above, the mid-rib a distinctive orange or yellow, but rusty tomentose below with a strong network of veins (reticulate). The primary veins are oblique and parallel and distinct on both surfaces.

Flowers: Flower spikes, 8–15 cm long by 7–8 cm wide, are a dark bluish-green (due to the colour of the perianth limbs) in their early stages but turn yellow-green as the flowers open. These are tipped black by the tiny pollen presenters at the ends of spreading styles, which are finally straight when released from the bottom of the spike first. As the flowers age they darken to a brownish-red or rust colour, which is similar to the rusty tomentum on the younger branches and leaves.

The flowering period seems to be spread over most months of the year.

Fruits: The cylindrical cones are roughly the same size as the flower spikes, the follicles villous, not thick, but protruding. The dead flowers remain for a few years before wearing away to reveal the follicles.

DISTRIBUTION: This swamp species is native to the sandy flats of the east coast of New South Wales and Queensland, apparently in three distinct populations from Wollongong north to South West Rocks; from Brunswick Heads to Rockhampton and from Cairns to Cooktown. Rainfall is 700 to more than 1250 mm spread throughout the year, but subject to heavy summer flooding.

CULTIVATION: It adapts to cultivation provided adequate moisture is given and the soil is on the acid side. Heavier soils do not appear to worry this shrub, particularly where sloping sites allow for extra drainage.

0 1 2 3 4 5
cm

B. saxicola A. S. George

GRAMPIANS BANKSIA

DESCRIPTION: Once considered a broad-leaved form of the Coast Banksia (*B. integrifolia*) which it resembles, this species is a spreading 3 m shrub without lignotuber, or sometimes in sheltered situations an erect, more slender tree to 13 m high. Bark is grey, smooth to rough, the younger branchlets densely tomentose becoming glabrous as they age.

The specific name is from the Latin *saxum* (a rock) and *-cola* (a dweller) and refers to the rocky habitat.

Leaves: These are a glossy leathery green above, white-tomentose below, 4–10 cm long by 1–4 cm wide, whorled, elliptic to obovate, entire, or sometimes with a few short lobes.

Flowers: The spikes are yellow with a grey tinge due to the grey, silky hairy perianth limbs. The styles are a smooth yellow and open from the bottom of the spike first. Flowering period is summer to early autumn.

Fruits: The withered flowers soon fall leaving a clean fruiting spike, the follicles at first densely furry, white or pale grey, but becoming smooth as they age. Some follicles open after a year or two and eject the seed, without requiring fire.

DISTRIBUTION: This species is restricted to the upper slopes of the Grampian Mountains and is also found on Wilsons Promontory in Victoria. It grows in loam among sandstone or granite boulders. Annual rainfall is 700–800 mm.

CULTIVATION: Little known in cultivation, it probably will adapt to heavier or stony soils where rainfall is assured to form a bushy shrub. Full sun or part shade would be best. Stratification of seed is necessary for germination. It has been successfully grown near Mount Gambier in South Australia in sandy loam.

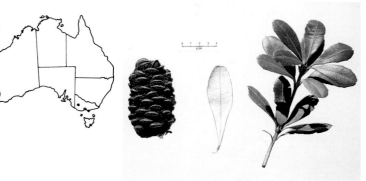

B. scabrella A. S. George

BURMA ROAD BANKSIA

DESCRIPTION: A sprawling shrub without a lignotuber, 1–2 m high and up to 3 m across, the lateral branches often resting on the ground. The young branchlets are white-tomentose.

The specific name refers to the leaves which are scabrid, i.e. rough to the touch.

Leaves: The leaves are crowded, narrowly linear, acute, normally 8–25 mm long by about 1 mm wide, and revolute. Their top surface is silky hairy becoming rough (scabrid) and the under-surface is woolly.

Flowers: The inflorescences are erect, ovoid to cylindrical, up to 6 cm long by about the same diameter. Perianths are silky hairy, mainly cream to pale yellow and styles smooth and yellow, although both perianths and styles become purplish towards the top of the flower spike. This gives the fully developed spike the colour effect of grading from creamy-yellow at the base to pale purple at the top. The styles remain permanently hooked after being released from the top of the spike first. Many inflorescences form at the ends of the lateral branches resting on the ground at the perimeter of the shrub.

The flowering period is spring to late summer, odd flowers appearing as late as April.

Fruits: The fruiting spike is similar in shape and size to the flower spike and supports many narrowly elliptic, mainly smooth follicles up to 30 mm long by 6–8 mm wide. The dead flowers persist for some time.

DISTRIBUTION: This species is one of restricted distribution, occurring in two separate populations east of Walkaway (south-east of Geraldton) and adjacent to Mt Adams (south-east of Dongara) in Western Australia. It favours sandy soil, sometimes over laterite. Annual rainfall is 450 mm.

CULTIVATION: Like many other banksias from Western Australia, *B. scabrella* is at its best in low nutrient sand where drainage is good. It has been grown successfully in light sand adjacent to Happy Valley Reservoir near Adelaide.

B. sceptrum Meisn.

SCEPTRE BANKSIA

DESCRIPTION: A spreading, but upright, dense and bushy shrub, sometimes a small tree, 2–5 m high, the foliage of glaucous appearance due to the dense, grey-white tomentum covering the younger branches and leaves. It has no lignotuber.

The specific name refers to the sceptre-like arrangement of the flower spikes on long branchlets.

Leaves: These are rigid, flat or undulate, oblong to oblong-cuneate, 3–9 cm long by about 2 cm wide, regularly dentate with small, shallow teeth, and blunt at the tips (truncate or emarginate). They are densely furry but soon wearing smooth, a dull blue or grey-green in colour, the mid-rib prominent and the venation reticulate on the under-surface.

Flowers: A distinctive feature of the erect flower spikes is the manner in which they are arranged at an oblique angle to the lateral branches. They are large and beautiful, cylindrical, 12–20 cm long by 8–12 cm in diameter, rich yellow or cream, with silky, hairy perianths. The long styles alternate with the flowers in single rows. They are released from the bottom of the spike first, and are characteristically bent. The pollen presenter is large, thick, and furrowed. At the bud stage the velvety red floral bracts contrast handsomely with the furry, white branches to which they are attached.

The flowering period is late spring and early summer.

Fruits: Cones are similar in shape and size to the flower spikes with prominent, furry, very thick seed follicles. The dead floral parts remain and partly obscure the follicles.

DISTRIBUTION: This northern sand plain species extends from Shark Bay south through the Murchison River and Mullewa areas to east of Geraldton, Western Australia. It grows in deep sands in open country with rainfall rarely exceeding 400 mm.

CULTIVATION: Although a dry area plant which is suited to hot, open, well-drained sites, this species is known to be successfully cultivated in cooler temperate areas with rainfall of 750 mm.

It grows fairly rapidly and flowers in three years from planting in slightly acid, sandy soils, but would probably also succeed in light, alkaline soils.

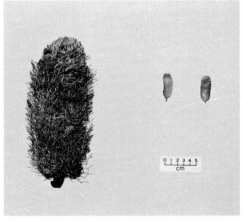

141

B. seminuda (A. S. George) B. L. Rye
subsp. *seminuda*
RIVER BANKSIA

DESCRIPTION: An erect, shapely, and extremely handsome tree at its best, with fresh green, luxuriant leaves, rough, dull grey bark and no lignotuber. It reaches heights of 20 m or more but is usually much shorter.

The specific name refers to the glabrous (or bare) limb of the perianth.

Leaves: These are narrowly elliptical-oblong, or broadly linear, 4–15 cm long by 1–2 cm wide, sometimes entire, but usually serrated with small, soft teeth over the full length of the leaf, or sometimes occurring only near the apex. The apexes are usually notched and truncate and the under-surface a soft, felted white. The leaves are arranged in whorls of four to six around the branchlets.

Flowers: Set in the forks between the branchlets, the erect, cylindrical flower spikes, up to 20 cm or more long by 4–7 cm in diameter, are yellow or yellowish-brown, due to the smooth yellow styles and silky hairy brownish-gold perianths. When the flowers open from the top of the spike first, the styles remain hooked and they subtend small, ovoid pollen presenters. There is a form with red styles.

The flowering period is late summer to winter.

Fruits: The fruiting cones are long, narrow, and cylindrical, the dead flowers soon falling to reveal numerous sharp, thin, protruding follicles. At first, both the follicles and the rachis are hoary tomentose, but they soon age to a smooth, dark grey.

DISTRIBUTION: An inhabitant of river banks and wet depressions of southern Western Australia between Banksiadale to Two Peoples Bay near Albany, sometimes in richer and heavier soils than those in which banksias are usually found. Rainfall is 900–1300 mm.

B. seminuda (A. S. George) B. L. Rye subsp. ***remanens*** Hopper. This is a shrubby form of the above species, also differing in its smaller, entire leaves with recurved margins, except for a few apical serrations, and its dense canopy of flowers, mainly in autumn and winter. The fruit bracts also feature narrowly elliptic, glabrous patches on their outer surface.

It is confined to a narrow band of the south coast of Western Australia, mainly in the Walpole–Nornalup National Park areas.

CULTIVATION: One of the most attractive of all the tree banksias because of its habit and foliage, it should grow well in a cool, temperate climate where there is an assured moisture supply and the soil is slightly acid, or neutral.

143

B. serrata L.f.

SAW BANKSIA, RED HONEYSUCKLE

DESCRIPTION: The Old Man Banksia of fairytale fame, this is one of the commonest species of the eastern States, where it is a large shrub, 3–8 m, or a single-stemmed tree, 10–16 m high. Typical of most tree banksias, it matures to a gnarled and crooked tree with a short, thick trunk, supporting many knotted and twisted, low-spreading branches. The bark is dark grey wearing to orange, rough and furrowed, and exudes a reddish, juicy sap. The timber is tough, beautifully grained, with good lasting qualities, and was once used in small-boat construction and for other purposes. It has a ligno-tuber and, after fire, sprouts from epicormic buds.

The specific name is derived from the serrated or saw-edged leaf margins.

Leaves: Mature leaves are large, 8–22 cm long by 2–4 cm wide, tough, leathery, and a glossy green, undulate or flat, usually with a greyish down on the under-surface, but sometimes glabrous on both surfaces. They are elliptic-oblong to narrowly obovate with coarsely, evenly serrated margins and parallel transverse veins. Young leaves are grey, soft, and hairy.

Flowers: 8–16 cm long by about 5–10 cm in diameter, the ovoid or cylindrical flower spikes are a lovely silvery-gold, due to the golden styles and silky grey (sometimes cream) perianth limb. The wiry yellow styles are released from the bottom of the spike first and are finally straight. As they wither they turn orange-red and then grey. The furrowed pollen presenter is 2 mm long and fusiform. In bud the flower spikes are a soft, velvety grey.

The flowering period is from late spring to early autumn.

Fruits: Embedded among the persistent flower remains, the large, thick, and hard follicles protrude prominently from the spike. They are ovate or rounded, 2–3 cm broad, and clad with a dense, velvety, grey tomentum.

DISTRIBUTION: Although found only at one isolated location in northern Tasmania (near Burnie), this species is well distributed throughout eastern Victoria from Wilsons Promontory; the coastal regions of New South Wales; the Blue Mountains and north to Fraser Island in Queensland. It favours poor sandy or rocky soils and is sometimes found as a sand binder in the hind dunes of the sea coast as well as at elevations. Rainfall is 700–1300 mm occurring throughout the year.

CULTIVATION: This species requires neutral to acid, well-drained soils with adequate moisture for success.

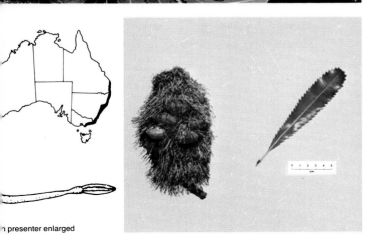

presenter enlarged

B. solandri R. Br.

SOLANDER'S BANKSIA, STIRLING RANGES BANKSIA

DESCRIPTION: A most decorative shrub because of its large, handsome, and distinctive leaves. It is normally an upright, open-branched shrub, 2–4 m high, although its rocky habitat is inclined to restrict its size under natural conditions. It has no lignotuber.

The specific name honours the Swedish botanist, D. C. Solander, who accompanied Joseph Banks on Cook's journey to Australia.

Leaves: Particularly ornamental, the oak-like leaves are 15–30 cm long by 6 cm or more wide, a smooth, dull green, but whitish on the under-surface, divided more than halfway to the mid-rib with large, rounded lobes of an irregular shape and size, and retuse at the apex. The margins are undulate, sometimes sinuate, slightly recurved. Veins are prominent on the under-surface, the yellow, rusty-hairy mid-rib very prominent, tapering to the apex from a short petiole.

Flowers: The flower spikes are more or less ovoid or cylindrical, 8–20 cm long by 6–10 cm in diameter, a rich, velvety, bronze colour. Perianths are hairy. The flowers on the spike are tightly compressed in a similar manner to the flowers of the prostrate *Banksia* species and there appears to be an affinity between *B. solandri* and these species. The styles, which are released from the bottom of the spike first, are finally straight and contain a very small pollen presenter.

Flowers occur in the spring months.

Fruits: These are significantly larger than the flower spikes, ovoid, up to 20 cm long by 8–10 cm in diameter, the hairy, rounded, and crowded follicles scarcely protruding from the thick, velvety spike. The dead, grey, floral parts remain on the spike.

DISTRIBUTION: This species is confined to the elevated and rocky slopes of the Stirling Ranges in Western Australia. Although the summer can be very dry with occasional heat waves, the climate is mainly cool due to the elevation. Rainfall is about 600 mm.

CULTIVATION: In cultivation this plant has shown that it likes cool situations, either in full sun or semi-shade. Provided that it is well-drained and not alkaline, the soil can be sand or heavy loam.

B. speciosa R. Br.

SHOWY BANKSIA

DESCRIPTION: A large, many-branched shrub, usually 3–5 m high with a spread of 2–3 m. Mature bark is grey, stippled, and slightly rough, but the younger branches are woolly white, grading to a very soft, velvety red bark on the very young branchlets. The long but narrow lobed leaves tend to create a wiry foliage effect. It has no lignotuber.

The specific name means 'showy' or 'handsome' and refers to the overall appearance of the shrub, particularly when in flower.

Leaves: These are 20–40 cm long by 1·5–2·5 cm wide, divided to the mid-rib by numerous triangular or dome-shaped lobes, flat or undulate, the margins revolute, a smooth dark green above but covered with a dense white tomentum on the reverse side. On the under-surface, conspicuous transverse veins converge to the slightly sharp-pointed apex of each lobe, and the mid-rib is very prominent. The young leaves are densely hairy.

Flowers: Set in a rosette of leaves, the erect, terminal flower spikes are large and conspicuous, usually about 12–15 cm long by almost the same in diameter. The new buds are a woolly white becoming a chartreuse colour, of almost conical shape, but later change to a citrus colour as the flowers open from the bottom of the spike upwards. Their eventual shape is squat, ovoid to oblong. The perianths are covered with long, soft hairs, the styles also hairy, rigid, with a narrow, furrowed pollen presenter, and curving slightly upwards as they are released.

The flowering period is summer and autumn and occasionally throughout the year.

Fruits: Roughly the same size and shape as the flower spikes with the dead flowers persistent, the fruiting cones enclose very large, densely furry, prominent follicles with a noticeable lip. At first the follicles are often like rich, red velvet, but turn dark brown and then grey as they age.

DISTRIBUTION: From the deep, sandy heathlands of the south coast of Western Australia, extending from Hopetoun to Israelite Bay with an outlier near Point Culver at the Great Australian Bight, this species can be seen in pure stands or sometimes accompanying the Water Bush (*B. occidentalis*). Rainfall is 400–500 mm.

CULTIVATION: This is a relatively easy shrub to grow in deep, well-drained, slightly acid-neutral, light soils and has occasionally been successful in heavier clay-loams.

B. sphaerocarpa R. Br.
var. *sphaerocarpa*

FOX BANKSIA, ROUND-FRUITED BANKSIA

DESCRIPTION: A widely distributed shrubby banksia from Western Australia. It is a shrub to 2 m high in the southern part of its range and to 50 cm in the north where it is often confused with *B. micrantha*. It has a lignotuber and usually many ascending branches at or near ground level.

The specific name refers to the spherical fruits.

Leaves: These are scattered dark green but rarely glaucous, narrowly linear, smooth, the apex pointed but not pungent and the margins revolute. Their length varies from 2–12 cm long and usually 1–1.5 mm broad.

Flowers: The flower spikes occur at the end of short lateral branches and are globular, 4–8 cm long by 6–9 cm wide, and a purplish-brown or brown colour. The styles remain permanently hooked when released. Perianths are silky hairy.

Flowering is variable, sometimes occurring throughout the year, but mainly from late summer to early winter.

Fruits: The spherical cones are larger than the flower spikes and profusely studded with prominent, rounded, but flat-topped follicles with a raised lip along the suture. These may be hidden by a tangled mass of dead floral parts.

DISTRIBUTION: In sand, often associated with laterite, it is found in the low woodland and shrublands of the south coast and Darling Plateau of Western Australia from near the Fitzgerald River National Park west to the Nannup area, including the Stirling Ranges, and north to the heathlands adjacent to Eneabba. Annual rainfall is 600–800 mm.

B. sphaerocarpa R. Br. var. *caesia* A. S. George. A variation differing in its mainly glaucous leaves, larger habit up to 4 m x 4 m, golden flowers and smaller follicles. It is found in two distinct areas, one east of New Norcia and the other in the central and southern wheatbelt from the Narrogin area east to beyond Hyden, growing in sand or sand over laterite. Previously considered not to overlap the range of var. *sphaerocarpa*, recent research shows an overlap near the boundary of the Stirling Range National Park. Annual rainfall is 350–450 mm. Flowering period is March to June.

B. sphaerocarpa R. Br. var. *dolichostyla* A. S. George. A variation differing from the other varieties in the longer perianths and longer styles. It has the larger habit, glaucous foliage and large golden flowers of var. *caesia*. The perianth limbs are bronze and silky hairy. It is restricted to ridge tops and flats in laterite gravel to the east of Hyden and Lake King. Annual rainfall is 300 mm. Flowering period is March to May.

CULTIVATION: All varieties of *B. sphaerocarpa* succeed in acid to neutral deep sand or sandy loam in an open situation.

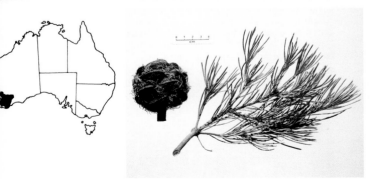

B. spinulosa Smith
var. *collina* (R. Br.) A. S. George
HILL BANKSIA

DESCRIPTION: Usually a medium-sized to large stiff shrub, 2–4 m high, with a lignotuber and smoothish grey-brown bark.

The varietal name is derived from the Latin *collinus*, meaning 'of hills' and referring to the hilly locality where Robert Brown first saw the species.

Leaves: The leaves are the main difference from *B. spinulosa* var. *spinulosa*, being wider (linear to narrowly obovate), usually with a blunt tip. They are flat, with recurved serrate margins and evident lateral veins.

Flowers: The cylindrical flower spikes, 5–20 cm long by 4–9 cm in diameter, are noted for the smooth and shiny, often black, yellow-tipped styles which remain permanently hooked as the flowers first open from the top of the spike. Style colour varies, however, both red and yellow occurring. Always attractive, the flower spikes arise from the centre of branch clusters and vary in colour from a honey-yellow to a purple-bronze, the perianths silky.

The flowering period is in autumn and winter.

Fruits: The cones are cylindrical, with thick, smooth, rounded follicles set in tight maize-like formation on the spike. The dead flowers persist where the follicles have not formed, but do not obscure the follicles.

DISTRIBUTION: A shrub of the open forest, woodland and heath in sand or loam. It extends along the east coast regions from Nambour in Queensland to the Hawkesbury River in New South Wales. Annual rainfall 600–1200 mm.

B. spinulosa Smith var. ***cunninghamii*** (Sieb. ex Reich) A. S. George. This variety differs in that it has no lignotuber and a generally taller (to 6 m) growth habit. The branchlets are hirsute and the leaves narrow to flat with serrate or entire margins, the undersurface a woolly pale brown (tomentose).

This variety is the southernmost occurrence in this group being common in Victoria from Wilsons Promontory and the Dandenongs east to the New South Wales border. It also occurs in New South Wales and north to the Lamington Plateau in Queensland. Annual rainfall 750–1200 mm.

CULTIVATION: Both varieties are relatively easy to grow provided the soil is well-drained, acid-neutral, and moisture is assured.

B. spinulosa Smith
var. *spinulosa*
HAIRPIN BANKSIA

DESCRIPTION: Hairpin Banksia is rarely more than a small or medium-sized divaricate shrub, although its size varies considerably according to conditions. The thin branches are clothed by a tomentum grading to a smoothish, grey-brown bark. It has a lignotuber.

The specific name is derived from the nature of the leaves, *spinulosa* meaning 'with small spines'.

Leaves: These are narrow-linear, 1–2 mm wide by 3–12 cm long, usually smooth above, and crowded. They are notched at the ends with a prominent point in the notch and several small teeth at this end, the margins very revolute. The fine, irregularly spaced serrations sometimes extend the full length of the leaf. Leaf variations occur but a white woolly under-surface is common.

Flowers: Several colour variations occur in the inflorescences from yellow to honey-bronze perianths and yellow, gold, red, or more commonly, black permanently hooked, smooth styles. These are first released from the top of the spike. The flower spikes are 5–20 cm long by 4–8 cm in diameter, the perianths pubescent.

The main flowering period is in autumn and winter when the freely produced flowers are a lovely sight.

Fruits: The cones are ovoid to cylindrical, the follicles glabrous but wrinkled, scarcely protruding from the spike, the dead flowers remaining where follicles have not formed.

DISTRIBUTION: Native to New South Wales, and Queensland, this shrub is widely distributed, extending as far as Mossman in northern Queensland south to near the Victorian border, mainly in open forest and woodland. Rainfall is 600–1400 mm.

CULTIVATION: One of the easier species to cultivate, Hairpin Banksia likes good drainage with adequate moisture, and neutral-acid soils.

B. spinulosa Smith var. *neoanglica* A. S. George. This lignotuberous variety, so named because of its main area of distribution — the New England Tableland of New South Wales — but it also occurs in the McPherson Range of southern Queensland and was first described in 1987.

It features entire, or toothed, slightly broader leaves than the preceding, with a pale brown to white tomentum on the under-surface, but no visible venation.

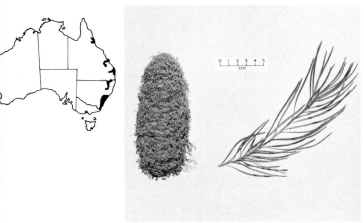

B. telmatiaea A. S. George

SWAMP FOX BANKSIA

DESCRIPTION: A usually erect shrub to 2 m high without a ligno-tuber. Bark is brownish and tomentose on the smaller branchlets. New growth is brownish, soon becoming green.

The specific name refers to the swampy habitat, meaning 'of a marsh' in Greek.

Leaves: These are narrowly linear, scattered, with obtuse to acute apexes and revolute margins. The upper surface is silky hairy becoming glabrous and the underside white tomentose.

Flowers: The flowering spikes are ovoid to cylindrical, occurring on short lateral branches. They are up to 8 cm long, width some-what less, a golden-brown to pale brown in colour. Perianths are hirsute outside and inside, the styles smooth and cream, remaining hooked after opening.

Flowering period is April to August.

Fruits: The spikes are roughly the same shape and size as the flowering spike, the old flowers persisting and surrounding numer-ous, narrowly elliptic, hairy follicles.

DISTRIBUTION: This is a swamp species, being found in deep, grey, sandy loam which is usually wet in winter. It occurs in shrubland or low woodland in Western Australia near the lower west coast between Badgingarra and Serpentine. Annual rainfall is 600–900 mm.

CULTIVATION: Although cultivation of this species is not well known to the authors it would appear to favour a wet situation (at least during winter months), preferably in full sun.

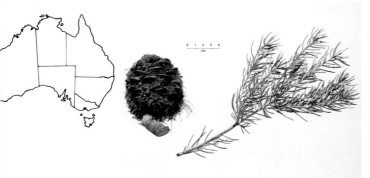

B. tricuspis Meisn.

PINE BANKSIA, LESUEUR BANKSIA

DESCRIPTION: This quite distinctive *Banksia* matures to a large, fairly open shrub up to 4 m high, but usually less, with fresh conifer-like foliage and marbled grey and brown mature bark. The bark is a smooth grey-brown on the younger branches. It has a lignotuber and after fire, shoots from epicormic buds.

The specific name refers to the notched tips of the leaves which are roughly three-pointed.

Leaves: Scattered and crowded, the narrow-linear leaves are 10–15 cm long by about 1·5 mm wide, a smooth, dull green above but with a white under-surface, the margins revolute almost to the mid-rib. Each leaf is notched at its apex so that it has one triangular point centrally in line with the mid-rib but is otherwise truncate, forming a three-pointed tip.

Flowers: The large, bright yellow, cylindrical flower spikes are 10–20 cm long by 8–10 cm in diameter. A somewhat unique feature is the habit of the very long (4 cm), permanently hooked, yellow styles to remain fresh for some time after the perianths have curled up, which gives the spike an open-textured, almost shaggy appearance, as the flowers age. The hairy perianths are about half the length of the styles, which are tipped by a small, brown, conical pollen presenter.

The flowering period is in autumn, winter, and early spring.

Fruits: The large, cylindrical cones, up to 20 cm or more long by 10–15 cm in diameter, rapidly shed the dead flowers to expose numerous, crowded, smooth follicles. At first these are bright emerald green but they soon age to a light grey colour. Set among the pine-like foliage they are a very ornamental feature of the plant.

DISTRIBUTION: This declared rare plant is restricted to a small area surrounding Mt Lesueur, north-east of Jurien Bay, in Western Australia, mainly in rocky lateritic soils on rocky hill tops, slopes, gullies and breakaways in low or tall shrublands. Annual rainfall is 600 mm.

CULTIVATION: This species requires a slightly acid to neutral, well-drained soil, but is successful in both light sand and heavier loam.

of leaf enlarged

159

B. verticillata R. Br.

ALBANY BANKSIA, GRANITE BANKSIA

DESCRIPTION: Probably due to its constant exposure to sea winds, this species is only found as a shrubby, or small tree form, growing among the rocky granite outcrops which occur in the Albany district of Western Australia. It has no lignotuber.

This shrub appears naturally as a thick-trunked, dome-shaped plant, 3–4 m high, growing in thickets among elevated rocks near the coast. An attractive feature of the plant is the white under-surface of the leaves which are prominently displayed in the windy conditions of its natural habitat.

The specific name refers to the leaf arrangement which is whorled around the stems (verticillate).

Leaves: These are narrowly elliptic to elliptical-oblong, 4–8 cm long by 1–2 cm wide, always entire and in whorls of four to six around the stems. The apex is rounded or obtuse, the margins are recurved and the under-surface a soft, felted white.

Flowers: The erect, cylindrical flower spikes are bright yellow, up to 25 cm long by 4–7 cm in diameter, set in the forks of the branches. Perianths are silky hairy, the brownish hairs giving the buds an appearance of burnished gold. The smooth, yellow styles remain partly hooked when released. The pollen presenter is small and ovoid.

The flowering period is late summer and autumn.

Fruits: The long, narrow, cylindrical fruiting cones soon shed the flowers to reveal numerous, thin, sharp, fairly small, deeply-embedded follicles. Both the fruits and the leaves bear a resemblance to the eastern species *B. integrifolia*.

DISTRIBUTION: Albany Banksia is a coastal plant found in two distinct areas, among the granite outcrops of the King George Sound area near Albany and at Walpole. Rainfall is about 850–1000 mm.

CULTIVATION: This species is a handsome small tree or shrub for garden culture in areas of high winter rainfall, acid to neutral soils, and a temperate climate. Where these conditions are encountered near the sea it should also be a very successful coastal plant.

B. victoriae Meisn.

WOOLLY ORANGE BANKSIA

DESCRIPTION: A medium to tall shrubby species, up to 6 m high, very often quite narrow in spread with few branches. It is noted for its very woolly foliage, particularly the soft, greenish to grey-white new leaf tips, and its hoary whitish branches. This plant has no lignotuber.

The specific name refers to Queen Victoria who reigned when much of the Australian flora was being named.

Leaves: These are identical in shape and size to those of *B. ashbyi* E. G. Bak. Their main difference is that they are very woolly-hirsute, particularly on the under-surface. They are long and narrow, flat or undulating, usually 15–30 cm long by 2–3 cm wide, and divided nearly to the mid-rib with sharp-tipped triangular lobes. The mid-rib is prominent on both surfaces and the venation distinct and reticulate on the under-surface, the transverse veins converging to the apex of each lobe.

Flowers: This is another species with orange and woolly-white acorn-shaped flower spikes when partly open. The upright spikes are terminal, 7–12 cm long by 7–8 cm in diameter, and set in a rosette of greyish leaves which enhance their attractiveness. Perianth tubes are softly hairy and bright golden yellow, the limb a very woolly-white before the flowers open. The styles which are smooth, bright orange, and erect when released, subtend darker orange, narrow, and furrowed pollen presenters.

The flowering period is in summer and autumn.

Fruits: These are roughly the same size and shape as the flower spikes. The follicles are densely furry, brown ageing to grey, mainly obscured by the persistent dead floral parts.

DISTRIBUTION: This is a shrub of the sandy heathlands of the Irwin district of Western Australia extending from Northhampton northwards to beyond the Murchison River. Rainfall is 350 mm.

CULTIVATION: *B. victoriae* is best suited to a warm, open, and well-drained site with slightly acid to slightly alkaline soil. It flowers at an early age.

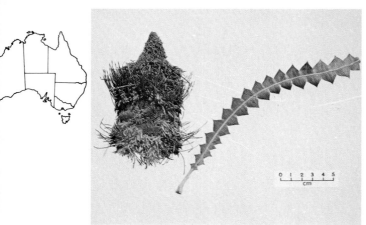

163

B. *violacea* C. A. Gardn.

VIOLET BANKSIA

DESCRIPTION: A small, many-branched shrub to about 1 m high and
wide, distinctive because of its unusual dark violet flowers. It has
glaucous, heath-like foliage and slender branches clothed with
smoothish grey-brown bark. Generally it has no lignotuber but
populations of plants with lignotubers have been recorded near
Woodanilling in Western Australia.

The specific name refers to the violet-coloured flowers.

Leaves: These are entire, smooth, narrow-linear, about 1.5–2 cm
long by 1.5 mm wide, bluish-green in colour, the margins revolute
to the mid-rib. The apex is pointed but not pungent.

Flowers: Numerous globular inflorescences, 6–8 cm in diameter,
appear on short lateral branches and are mainly set within the foliage. The long hooked styles are a dark metallic violet, or almost
black, and glisten beautifully in sunlight. Perianths are villous and
the pollen presenter conical.

Flowers mainly occur from late summer to mid-winter.

Fruits: The roughly globular fruiting cones are larger than the
flower spikes (9–10 cm in diameter) with many tightly compressed,
dark grey, hairy follicles. The follicles are more or less wedge-
shaped, flatish on top with a conspicuous suture, but scarcely
protruding. The dead flowers remain for a short time but soon fall.

DISTRIBUTION: This is a well-distributed shrub of the sandy soils
sometimes over laterite and extending from the wheatbelt areas of
Woodanilling eastwards to Esperance, in Western Australia. It is a
common plant along the Esperance–Ravensthorpe road. Rainfall is
300–500 mm, mainly in winter.

CULTIVATION: This species requires well-drained slightly acid soils
and assured winter moisture for best results. It grows well on the
sandy soils of South Australia's south-east.

BIBLIOGRAPHY

AUSTRALIAN PLANTS, Journal of the Society for Growing Australian Plants, Vol. 5, No. 41, December 1969 and Vol. 5, No. 43, June 1970 (Sydney).

BAGLIN, D. & MULLINS, B., *Australian Banksias*. Horwitz Publications (North Sydney, 1970).

BAILEY, F. M., *The Queensland Flora Part IV*. Diddams (Brisbane, 1901).

BEADLE, N. C. W., EVANS, O. D., & CAROLIN, R. C., *Flora of the Sydney Region*. Reed (Sydney, 1973).

BEARD, J. S. (ed.), *West Australian Plants*. The Society for Growing Australian Plants (Sydney, n.d.).

BENTHAM, G., *Flora Australiensis*. Reeve (London, 1863–78).

BLACKALL, W. E. & GRIEVE, B. J., *How to Know Western Australian Wildflowers*, 2nd Ed., University of Western Australia Press, Perth (1980).

BOOMSMA, C. D., *Native Trees of South Australia*. Bulletin No. 19, Woods & Forests Department (Adelaide, 1972).

CONRAN, J. G. & CLIFFORD, H. T., *Variation in Banksia oblongifolia* Cav. (Proteaceae) *Brunonia 10*, 2:177–187. (1987).

CURTIS, WINIFRED M., *The Students Flora of Tasmania, Part 3*. Government Printer (Hobart, 1967).

ERICKSON, RICA, GEORGE, A. S., MARCHANT, N. G. & MORCOMBE, M. K., *Flowers and Plants of Western Australia*. Reed (Sydney, 1973).

FAIRALL, A. R., *West Australian Native Plants in Cultivation*. Pergamon Press (Rushcutters Bay, N.S.W., 1970).

GARDNER, C. A., *Wildflowers of Western Australia*. West Australian Newspaper (Perth, 1945, 1959).

GEORGE, A. S., *The Banksia Book*, 2nd Ed. Kangaroo Press in association with the Society for Growing Australian Plants — N.S.W. Ltd. (Sydney, 1987).

GEORGE, A. S., *The Genus Banksia* L.f. (Proteaceae) *Nuytsia 3*, 3:239–473, Government Printer, Western Australia (1981).

HOLLIDAY, IVAN, *A Field Guide to Australian Trees*. 2nd Ed. Rigby Hamlyn (Melbourne, 1989).

JESSOP, J. P. & TOELKEN, H. R. (eds), *Flora of South Australia*, 4th Ed., S.A. Government Printer, Adelaide (1986).

LEBLER, BERYL A., *Banksias of South-eastern Queensland*. Reprinted from Queensland Agricultural Journal, July 1972, Advisory Leaflet No. 1157, Dept of Primary Industries (Brisbane, 1972).

MAIDEN, J. H., *The Forest Flora of New South Wales, Vols. I–VIII*. Government Printer (Sydney, 1904).

NEWBEY, KEN, *West Australian Plants for Horticulture, Part I*. The Society for Growing Australian Plants (Sydney, 1968).

ROGERS, F. J. C., *Growing Australian Native Plants*. Thomas Nelson (Melbourne, 1971).

TAYLOR, A. & HOPPER, S. D. *Banksia Atlas*, Government Printer, Western Australia (1984).

TAYLOR, A. & HOPPER, S. D., *The Banksia Atlas*. Australian Government Publishing Service, Canberra (1988).

WILLIS, J. H., *A Handbook to Plants in Victoria, Vol. II*. Melbourne University Press (Melbourne, 1972).

GLOSSARY

acute: sharp, sharply pointed at an acute angle.

acuminate: an acuminate apex is finely tapered.

alternate: arising at different levels — referring to the position of successive leaves on the branchlets.

anther: the pollen-bearing part of a stamen.

appendage: an attached secondary part.

apex: the tip of an organ, such as a leaf.

aristate: tapering to a long narrow point — e.g. the tip of a leaf (also means bearing a stiff bristle or bristle-like awn).

awn: a fine bristle-like appendage.

bract: a leaf-like structure beneath a flower or flower head.

bracteole: a small bract immediately below the calyx of a flower.

capsule: a dry fruit consisting of more than one carpel usually splitting into valves when ripe to liberate the seeds.

carpel: the female reproductive part of a flower which bears the ovary.

conical: cone-shaped.

corolla: the whole of the petals of a single flower.

cuneate: wedge-shaped.

cuneate-oblong: shaped roughly halfway between cuneate and oblong (referring to the shape of the leaves).

cylindrical: shaped like a cylinder with both sides more or less parallel.

deflexed: bent downwards.

dentate: with saw-like teeth on the margin, the teeth pointing outwards (referring to leaves).

denticulate: dentate, but with the teeth much reduced.

divaricate: branching widely, spreading.

elliptic: shaped like an ellipse (referring to the shape of the leaves).

elliptical-oblong: shaped roughly halfway between elliptic and oblong.

emarginate: with a small notch at the apex.

entire: without toothing or divisions (referring to leaves).

epicormic buds: those that are normally dormant but are capable of developing to a shoot after a growth stimulus (e.g. regrowth after fire).

falcate: sickle-shaped; flat, curving, and tapering to a point.

follicle: a dry fruit containing more than one seed which splits open along one side only — e.g. a banksia fruit.

fusiform: spindle-shaped; circular in cross-section, broadest at the centre, and tapered evenly to each end.

glabrous: smooth, without hairs.

glaucous: bluish-green, with a powdery bloom.

globular: rounded or ball-shaped.

hirsute: covered with long stiff hairs.

hoary: whitish-grey; covered with short, dense, greyish hairs.

incurved: turned or bent inwards — e.g. the styles of some banksias.

inflorescence: the flower-bearing system — e.g. the complete flower spike of a banksia.

laminae: refers to the flattened part of an organ — e.g. the limbs or segments of the perianths of a banksia flower.

lanceolate: shaped like the head of a lance, tapering at both ends, but broadest slightly below the middle.

lateral: occurring at the side.

lateritic: of a soil, containing laterite or ironstone.

lignotuber: a conspicuous woody swelling at or below soil level which can produce new shoots and roots as after a fire.

linear: long and narrow with more or less parallel sides.

lobe: the segments or divisions of a structure — e.g. some leaves are divided into several lobes.

margin: the edge of a leaf.

mid-rib: the main central vein of a leaf.

narrow-elliptic: ellipse-shaped, but much narrower than normal (referring to the shape of the leaves).

obcordate: inversely heart-shaped (i.e. with a broad, shallowly notched apex).

oblanceolate: inversely lanceolate or lance-shaped; the broadest section (referring to a leaf) being above the middle.

oblique: slanting or with unequal sides.

oblong: with sides more or less parallel except at the base and the apex.

oblong-cylindrical: cylinder-shaped with the sides nearly parallel except at the base and the apex (a common shape for the flower spikes or the fruiting cones of many banksias).

obovate: inversely ovate; egg-shaped, with the narrow end at the bottom (referring to the shape of a leaf).

ovary: the part of the flower containing the ovules which, when fertilised, becomes the fruit.

ovate: egg-shaped in profile, and broadest below the mid-line (referring to the shape of a leaf).

ovoid: egg-shaped, the broadest part below the mid-line (referring to a solid part of a plant — e.g. the fruit).

obovate-oblong: shaped approximately halfway between obovate and oblong (referring to the shape of the leaves).

perianth: the collective term for the calyx and corolla of a flower; particularly applicable to many Proteaceae — e.g. banksia flowers.

perianth limb: the flattened, expanded part of a perianth, the base of which is tubular — e.g. the tips of the perianths of a banksia flower.

perianth tube: the lower tubular part of a perianth joining its limb to the ovary.

petiole: the stalk of a leaf.

pistil: the female organ of a flower consisting of ovary, style and stigma (and pollen presenter in Proteaceae). It may consist of one carpel, when it is a simple pistil (as in *Banksia* species) or of two or more carpels, in which case it is a compound pistil.

pinnatifid: of a leaf, having lobes cut near to the mid-rib — e.g. some forms of the leaves of *Banksia repens*.

pollen presenter: the part of a style on which pollen is placed just before the flower opens and which 'presents' it for a visiting pollinator.

primary veins: the major vein structure of a leaf.

pubescent: covered with short soft or silky hairs.

pungent: terminating in a stiff, sharp point.

rachis: the primary axis of an inflorescence, or a compound leaf.

recurved: curving backwards or downwards.

reflexed: bent or turned sharply backwards — e.g. the leaves of *Banksia meisneri.*

rendzina soils: shallow, residual soils developed on calcareous or limestone rock. Rendzinas are characteristically dark in colour (black or dark brown); cf. terra rossa soils which are red.

reticulate: forming a network; usually referring to secondary veins in a leaf.

retuse: having a narrow, shallow notch or curve in an obtuse apex (referring to the tip of a leaf).

revolute: with the margins or apex rolled backwards.

scabrid: rough to the touch.

sclerophyll forest: a forest community dominated by evergreen sclerophyllous trees (trees with hard-textured leaves such as *Eucalyptus*).

serrated: with forward-pointing teeth, like a saw.

sessile: without a stalk.

sinuate: with a wavy margin due to shallow lobing.

spike: an arrangement of unstalked flowers attached directly to a common axis — e.g. the flowers of banksias.

stigma: the part of a carpel which receives the pollen. In *Banksia* it is a small groove in the style end or pollen presenter.

style: the slender part of a carpel connecting a stigma to its ovary.

suture: the line of junction of two united parts.

terete: needle-like; shaped like a slender shaft.

terra rossa soils: shallow residual soils developed on calcareous or limestone rock, and red or reddish-brown in colour.

tomentose (noun tomentum): covered with dense woolly hairs.

undulate: wavy (up and down in a different plane).

valve: the segment of a fruit which naturally opens at maturity, usually releasing seeds.

vein: the strand of conducting tissue in the structure of a leaf.

venation: the way in which veins are arranged.

verticillate: arranged in radial formation, or in rings around the nodes.

villous: covered with long soft hairs.

whorled: verticillate; arranged in radial formation around an axis.

LEAVES

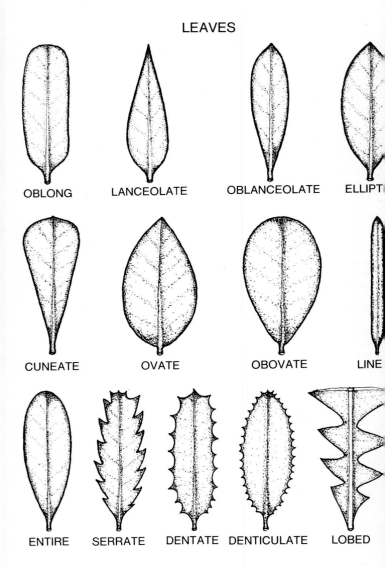

OBLONG   LANCEOLATE   OBLANCEOLATE   ELLIPT

CUNEATE   OVATE   OBOVATE   LINE

ENTIRE   SERRATE   DENTATE   DENTICULATE   LOBED

APEX SHAPES

truncate   retuse   obtuse   acute   acuminate   aristate   emarg

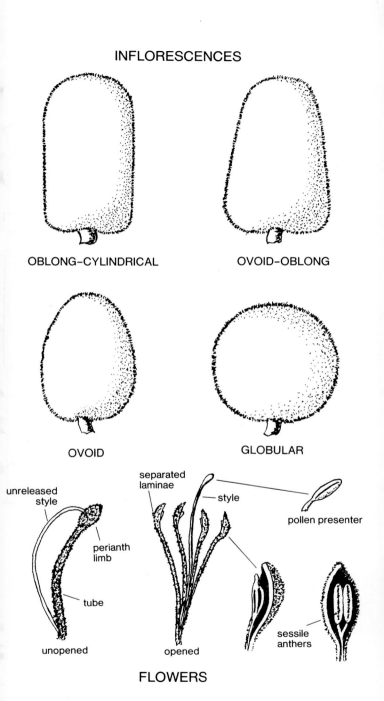

INFLORESCENCES

OBLONG–CYLINDRICAL

OVOID–OBLONG

OVOID

GLOBULAR

unreleased style

separated laminae

style

pollen presenter

perianth limb

tube

unopened

opened

sessile anthers

FLOWERS

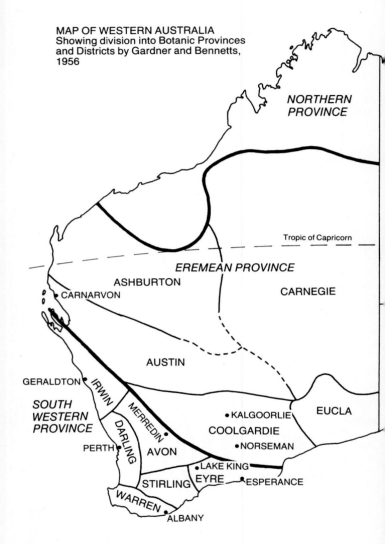

MAP OF WESTERN AUSTRALIA
Showing division into Botanic Provinces
and Districts by Gardner and Bennetts,
1956

NORTHERN PROVINCE

Tropic of Capricorn

EREMEAN PROVINCE

ASHBURTON

CARNARVON

CARNEGIE

AUSTIN

GERALDTON

IRWIN

SOUTH WESTERN PROVINCE

MERREDIN

DARLING

PERTH

AVON

KALGOORLIE

COOLGARDIE

NORSEMAN

EUCLA

LAKE KING

STIRLING

EYRE

ESPERANCE

WARREN

ALBANY

Index of Common Names

INDEX OF SCIENTIFIC NAMES